Words About Fast Track

"This was the last piece of the puzzle for me. Until I read Fast Track, *I had been postponing too many very important decisions."*

> STEVE DECHIARA
> Founder and President
> OnDisc, Inc.

"The message here is powerful and practical. It shows me how to take action in many areas I was guessing about but had no clear direction to complete."

> GENE FRENCH
> Founder and President
> Quote Me, Inc.

"I've been waiting a long time for someone to show why commitment or dedication are only the starting point for success. This is it!"

> STEVE TAKAHASHI
> Principal
> Plus Software, Inc.

Other Books by Roger Fritz

What Managers Need to Know

Productivity and Results

Performance Based Management

Rate Yourself as a Manager

You're in Charge: A Guide for Business and Personal Success

The Inside Advantage

Nobody Gets Rich Working for Somebody Else

Personal Performance Contracts

If They Can—You Can! Lessons from America's New Breed of
Successful Entrepreneurs

Rate Your Executive Potential

Management Ideas That Work

How to Export: Everything You Need to Know to Get Started

Ready, Aim, HIRE! (Co-author)

The Entrepreneurial Family: How to Sustain the Vision and Value in
Your Family Business

Think Like a Manager

Sleep Disorders: America's Hidden Nightmare

Sales Manager's High Performance Guide: The Only Reference You
Need to Build a Powerful Sales Force

A Team of Eagles

How to Manage Your Boss

The Small Business Troubleshooter

Wars of Succession

America Behind Bars: Bold New Ways to Fit Punishment With Crime

One Step Ahead, The Unused Keys to Success

Bounce Back and Win: What It Takes and How To Do It

On CD-ROM

The Personal Business Coach, (CD-ROM)

Beyond Commitment: The Skills All Leaders Need

ROGER FRITZ

Inside Advantage
Naperville, Illinois

Published by Inside Advantage
1240 Iroquois Drive, Suite 406
Naperville, IL 60563
P. 630-420-7673
F. 630-420-7835
rfritz3800@aol.com
www.rogerfritz.com

Design by Patrick J. Falso, Allegro Design Inc.
Printed by Publishers' Graphics, LLC

02 01 00 99   5 4 3 2 1

Printed in the United States of America

Contents

Introduction 1

Chapter 1—Do You Really Know Yourself 3
   Role Modeling for Yourself 4
   Personal Due Diligence 5
   Leave Your Ego on the Doorstep 6
   Your Credibility Quotient 8
   RX: Prescription for Change 10
   When It's Time to Change…Don't Wait Too Long 13
   Solo or Symphony? 15

Chapter 2—Any Dream Won't Do 17
   A Formula That Fits Every Need 19
   Top Car Seller Works at Home 19
   Positive Thinking Isn't Enough 20
   Why Good People Burn Out 23
   Winners Build—Losers Blame 24

Chapter 3—Easy Doesn't Do It 27
   No Silver Bullets (the Lone Ranger Took Them All) 27
   Make Yourself Needed 29
   Get Up—Move On 30
   Failure or Mismatch? 32
   Make Your Own Path 33
   Write Your Own Epitaph—I Dare You! 33
   The Ultimate Compliment 34

Contents

Chapter 4—A Reverence for Work *35*
    Why Work? 35
    Is a College Degree the Answer? 40
    The Busyness Trap 41
    Are You Referenceable? 42
    Thinking: The Hardest Work There Is 44
    Mind Scars 45

Chapter 5—How to Be a Rainmaker *47*
    Strong Bow, Empty Quiver—The Value of Being Prepared 50
    Be Your Own Mentor 51
    Manipulating Minutia 52
    Don't Waste Time On Yesterday 53
    Excellent Excuses 55
    Information—Power or Burden? 58
    Don't Build Fences Within Your Mind 59
    Attitude Makes the Difference 60
    Who Is Your Prompter? (It Better Be You) 61

Chapter 6—The Power of Persistence *63*
    It's Better to Avoid Dragons Than to Slay Them 64
    Coping With Failure 65
    The Fine Art of Hunkering 69
    The Source of Power 72

Chapter 7—Living Above Fear *75*
    When Will You Flinch 76
    Why Losers Lose 79
    Traveling Light: The Simpler the Better 83
    Why Bad Things Happen to Good People 83
    Unacceptable Guilt 84
    Get a Life 85

Chapter 8—Victim of Success *87*
    Behold the Naked Monarch 89
    Andrew Carnegie Revisited 91
    Whole Lotta Cheatin' Goin' On—Don't Get Caught Up In It 92
    Don't Let Competition Decide 93
    When Greed Prevails 93

Contents

Chapter 9—What Good Is Experience? *95*
   Dependence Is Not Dependable 101
   Planning Puts Experience in Focus 102
   No Short Cuts 104
   Use It or Lose It 106
   Send Me In, Coach 108
   Get the Wind at Your Back 111

Chapter 10—The Secrets of Self Mastery *113*

About the Author 121

Index 123

Acknowledgment

The involvement in this project of Don Young is deeply appreciated. He not only shares my convictions in many of the key areas examined, he has also been a persistent analyst of some very controversial issues and a most constructive critic.

Introduction

Some people will *never* consider themselves successful. No matter how much money they make or what lofty rank they attain, they will never take the time to define what "success" means to them.

Success means different things to different people. Your definition of success can only be made by you. It requires honesty, objectivity and a lot of soul-searching. The answer will be found not in "What will make me successful?" but "What will make me satisfied, happy and fulfilled."

After a two-year search for living examples of sustained career momentum, I discovered the best a few days before this book was sent to the printer when my wife and I went to a concert featuring Patti Page. Known as the "Singing Rage" in the 1940's, she has released more than 100 albums and 160 singles in a career that has spanned five decades. She has three gold albums and 15 gold singles including the hits "Old Cape Cod," "Allegheny Moon" and " Doggie In The Window." Her biggest hit, "Tennessee Waltz," sold more than 10 million copies and is the largest-selling single by a female artist. With more than 100 million records sold to date, Patti Page is still the all-time best-selling female vocalist.

Born Clara Ann Fowler in Claremore, Oklahoma, one of her earliest recollections include walking barefoot to school and saving her one pair of shoes for Sunday dress-up. With a solid talent and sheer perseverance she became a sophisticated and sensitive performer with a 60-year career spanning nightclubs, concert halls, the musical comedy stage, motion pictures, radio and television.

Now 77 years old, her voice is clear, audiences love her and she still does over 40 concerts each year. Her secret—she knows what she's good at, she likes to do it and that fact is obvious to everyone who sees and hears her sing.

A career "road map" will help you to plan a *realistic* future. The first step is to set attainable targets en route to your objective. These "checkpoints" can be as helpful to you in pursuing a career as they are to a motorist who is heading for a strange city. They keep you on course and let you know that you're making progress. They provide you with encouragement every time a new checkpoint is reached. They keep you from feeling discouraged, and provide new momentum to spur you on toward the next objective.

- Reaching each new checkpoint reassures you that you ARE on track, that you CAN make it, and that you WILL succeed if you keep going.
- Checkpoint planning also helps make time pass more quickly, because progress is measured in a smaller scale.

This book is about momentum—the forces that will keep you moving forward. Actually, it is a series of personal challenges. None are guaranteed to be easy. All *are* guaranteed to be understandable and reliable ways to get on the fast track and have the momentum to stay there.

—Roger Fritz

C H A P T E R   1

Do You Really Know Yourself?

When assessing career possibilities, it is not enough to determine what we want to be. It is vital to recognize and then evaluate what we truly are now.

I learned that valuable lesson several years ago when I became president of a university. After a few years, I discovered that wasn't really what I wanted after all. The job fell far short of providing the satisfactions I had expected. Looking back, I wish I had known about what Warren Bennis (who was also serving as a university president at that time) calls his four-point test for anyone anxious to achieve "success":

1. Try to discover what drives you and what gives you satisfaction.
2. See if there is a difference between what you want and what you're good at.
3. Clarify your values and priorities, and determine whether they are different from your employer's.
4. After gauging the differences between what you want and what you do well, and the differences be-

tween what *drives* you and what *satisfies* you, you must decide honestly and objectively whether you are capable of overcoming those differences.

In most cases, what we do and how we do it defines who we are. For Daniel Snyder, president and CEO of Snyder Communications, Inc., in Bethesda, Maryland, "success" isn't just about making money. He says it's also about proving to himself—and to others—that he can *do what he sets out to do* and that he can *create something that really matters.*

Role Modeling for Yourself

Nobody should know you better than you know yourself. The key is objectivity—the ability to analyze yourself and your desires dispassionately. Small children watch famous athletes like Michael Jordan, Mark McGwire, and Tiger Woods and say "I want to be just like him." As we get older, we know better. It is no less realistic to say, "I want to be like Bonnie Blair" than it is to say, "I want to be like Bill Gates." We are what we are: each of us is endowed with our own set of interests, skills, and abilities. The idea is to determine how to invest those resources to best advantage, how to channel our efforts, and how to excel at *whatever* we elect to do.

John Mackey is founder and CEO of Whole Foods Market in Austin, Texas, the country's largest natural foods grocer, with nearly a billion dollars a year in revenues. His outlook is simple, he:

1. Never allows himself to become a victim of anyone else.

2. Makes decisions based upon which alternative creates the most excitement within his own mind and heart.
3. Does what he's afraid to do until it doesn't frighten him anymore.
4. Tries to live each day as an adventure.

Robert Dunn, president and CEO of Business for Social Responsibility in San Francisco, believes that success in business, success in dealing with other people, and success in helping to improvement the community are all dependent, in large measure, on exercising personal integrity and on treating other people with respect.

"Don't concentrate on making a lot of money. Concentrate instead on becoming the type of person that people want to do business with. *Then* you will most likely make a lot of money," adds Patricia Fripp. Fripp ought to know. In 1969, while working in a hotel beauty shop in San Francisco, she began to deliver speeches to groups of local hairdressers, Rotary Clubs, and Bay-area Kiwanis Clubs. Soon she began to speak to larger groups and draw larger fees. By 1984, Fripp had become the first woman to be elected president of the National Speakers Association.

Personal Due Diligence

Success *doesn't just happen*. It comes about as the result of exercising due diligence in working your way up the ladder, in doing your job and doing it well, and in helping others do their work well.

Layne Longfellow believes that "Success is in the journey, not in the destination." Think about it. Many high-level positions are occupied by people who inherited their offices by virtue of their parents' achievements rather than their own. Does that qualify as "success" according to your standards?

Money, too, can be inherited, or won in a state lottery, but few people would consider those who achieve their wealth by those means to be "successful." Personal success stems from only one source: you!

Author and former NFL football official Jim Tunney puts it this way: "Winners don't have a positive attitude because they win. They win because they have a positive attitude."

Another author, Richard Leider of Scandia, Minnesota, thinks good career decisions can be worked out according to a formula: $(T+P+E) \times V$. In Leider's equation, T = Talent, P = Passion or Purpose, E = one's work Environment, and V = Vision. If you apply your Vision of your work and your career to the combination of the Talent, Passion, and Environment in which you have to work, you can do your best work and attain your highest level of success.

In reality, life is anticipation, and success is not an event but a series of increasingly difficult accomplishments. In fact, I believe that:

> *Momentum is gained by focusing on what remains to be done, not by focusing on past accomplishments.*

Leave Your Ego on the Doorstep

The most glaring omission in the lives of real leaders is ego. It is also the single greatest stumbling block for those who aspire to lead. It prevents people from seeing situations clearly and dispassionately. It divides people and destroys attempts at teamwork. It puts "Me" above "We" and the feelings of dominant single individuals above the search for a common goal.

But if *ego* inhibits group progress, it should not be confused with *pride*.

Pride is as *valuable* as ego is *harmful*. Pride ensures that we will make every possible effort to do as well as we possibly can. Pride underlies virtue, integrity, ambition, and honesty.

> *If you like confidentiality, spend your time with egotists. They only talk about themselves.*

Pride, even more than money, is one of life's prime motivators. Pride should be *encouraged*. Ego should be *dis*couraged.

Charles Handy, an author residing in London, England, illustrates the difference between pride and ego with an example from his own life.

Handy's father was a quiet, modest man who had lived most of his life in the Irish countryside. He served as the minister of a small church and lived a simple life.

His son, however, had become a professor at the London Business School, had written numerous magazine articles and best-selling business books, and often jetted around the world lecturing at major universities and consulting for big-name companies. He became, by his own admission, something of a "hotshot."

Then Handy's father died.

Handy flew to Ireland to attend his father's funeral and marveled at the number of people who came from all over the British Isles to attend the affair. Many of them went up to Handy to tell him how much his father had influenced their lives.

Standing by his father's grave, Handy wondered how many people would be interested in attending *his* funeral, how many lives *he* had touched in his brilliant, high-profile career.

When he returned to London, Handy resigned his professorship at the London Business School and dropped the pretense of being someone other than who he was. "I stopped trying to be a hotshot," he says, "and decided to do what I could to make a genuine difference in other people's lives."

There is another interesting benefit to setting aside ego in the pursuit of success: Nobody in baseball bats a thousand; nobody in tennis delivers an ace on every serve; nobody in business goes through an entire career without mistakes. For accomplishers—particularly those who are attempting to do something different, new, or special—an occasional failure is to be expected.

Ego prevents us from admitting that we are even *capable* of failure. To do a job better than it is currently being done requires experimenting with alternatives. Everyone makes mistakes, everyone looks foolish sometimes. Whenever my wife discovers me inflating my ego balloon, she punctures it and the hot air escapes harmlessly. Bless her for that! Without it, I would no doubt be a hopeless bore.

Your Credibility Quotient

Our ability to lead, to achieve life goals, to become successful at almost any level, depends in large part on our credibility. If coworkers cannot rely on us, if customers cannot trust us, we will fail.

People must believe that what you say is accurate, that you can and will do what you say you will do—that *you can be trusted.*

J. C. Watts, a Congressman who represents the Fourth District of Oklahoma, learned a lesson about credibility when he played football in high school. While reviewing a rival team's films before an important game, Watts's coach stopped the projector to call attention to the numerous "trick plays" that the team was employing.

"When a team runs that many 'gadget plays,'" the coach told his team, "you can assume that it's covering up for a weakness. Find that weakness and you can defeat the team."

> *Nothing is particularly hard if you divide it into small jobs.*—Henry Ford

As quarterback for the University of Oklahoma, Watts used that lesson to lead his team to two consecutive Big Eight championships as well as two consecutive Orange Bowl victories. He was voted into the Orange Bowl Hall of Honor. The victories did not come from trickery; they were the result of credibility and persistence.

Here is a starting point to help you assess where you are now, where you want to go, and how you expect to get there. Use it to begin creating the momentum you will need, and remember, if you don't write down your commitments, you aren't likely to keep them. Why? Because the faintest ink is better than the finest memory!

RX: Prescription for Change

What Do I Like *Most* About My Life?

At work?

_____

_____

_____

At home?

_____

_____

_____

What Do I Like *Least* About My Life?

At work?

_____

_____

_____

At home?

_____

_____

_____

How Did I Get to This Point?

At work?

Critical Decisions	When Made

At home?

Critical Decisions	When Made

What Would I Most Like to Change?

At work?

Change	Why?	When?

At home?

Change	Why?	When?

If These Changes Are Made, What Outcomes/Results Are Likely?

Outcome/Result	When?	Reason

Would These Results Be What I Really Want?

☐ Yes,

because _____

_____

_____

☐ No,

because _____

_____

_____

What Help Do I Need to Get the Results I Want?

Help Needed	Helper(s)

When Will I Ask Them?

Why Don't You Do Something?

"On the street I saw a girl cold and shivering in a thin dress, with little hope of a decent meal. I became angry and said to God: 'Why did You permit this? Why don't You do something about it?' For a while God said nothing. That night He replied quite suddenly: 'I certainly did something about it. I made you.'"

When It's Time to Change . . . Don't Wait Too Long!

One of the oldest clichés known to man is "nothing is permanent but change." It sticks because it's true. But how do we know when it's time to change? Everyday life can give us powerful clues. Check whether you are innocent, guilty, or undecided:

It's time to change when:	I am Innocent	I am Guilty	Undecided
Facts don't match my favorite opinions.	☐	☐	☐
Trusted friends and relatives say I am wrong.	☐	☐	☐
I am surprised that my time-tested methods aren't working.	☐	☐	☐
I am shocked that someone I have greatly admired has accepted an idea I have long opposed.	☐	☐	☐
My boss hints that one of my favorite duties will be assigned to someone else.	☐	☐	☐
A competitor exploits a weakness I have not acknowledged.	☐	☐	☐
I realize that I haven't set challenging personal goals for several years.	☐	☐	☐
I realize that younger people have been promoted to positions I wanted.	☐	☐	☐
It dawns on me that I am computer illiterate.	☐	☐	☐
I acknowledge that I have trusted seniority more than performance.	☐	☐	☐
I catch myself defending job entitlements in business and the tenure system in education.	☐	☐	☐
I lose my temper with one of my kids for doing something they learned from me.	☐	☐	☐
I get angry with my spouse for reminding me of a bad habit I can't seem to break.	☐	☐	☐
Someone else has to finish most of the projects I start.	☐	☐	☐
My past jobs have been replaced by machines or computers.	☐	☐	☐

Scoring Key

0–4 Guilty pleas:	You are adapting well to change.
5–10 Guilty pleas:	You are in serious danger of falling behind.
11–15 Guilty pleas:	You have waited too long to change. Drastic action is needed.

Note: If you checked "undecided" four or more times, you are likely to be manipulated frequently.

Solo or Symphony?

A symphony orchestra is composed of talented musicians who could each be soloists but have learned to combine their talents to produce beautiful music in harmony. Success requires *both* individual performance and teamwork. Performance begins with competence and expertise. Teamwork begins with an understanding of each member's behavior, especially in pressure situations.

CHAPTER 2

Any Dream Won't Do

Successful people follow their dreams. But "any old dream" won't do. Think about it: There is a certain maturity sequence to our dreams. We have small dreams and big dreams. We have short-range dreams and long-range dreams. We have romantic dreams, financial dreams, career and vocation dreams.

We begin dreaming at an early age, and our dreams reflect that immaturity. In those early years, we dream about a new bicycle, a doll, a trip. As we get a little older, we dream about being able to stay up past 10 o'clock . . . about reaching an age when we can drive a car . . . about having a date with the most popular guy or girl in class . . . about being a star athlete, or about getting good grades in school.

The key to success is in not allowing small problems to get big.

Our dreams become stronger and much more complex as we become adults. Marriage. A family. A nice home and a car. A good job. Respect.

Can you imagine being successful without first having earned the respect of those with whom you associate? It can't be done. It may be that some do not *like* you, but they all must *respect* you. **True success and respect are inseparably linked.**

And so we return to the matter of fulfilling our dreams as a means of achieving success.

To be successful, we first must dream of achieving a commendable goal. Then we must couple that dream with a reality—gaining the respect of associates. Given those two ingredients, can we be certain that we will become successful? No, it is only the starting point. Hard work must now be applied.

Most of our values are instilled in us by our parents while we are children. Our development involves how well we absorb those values, analyze them, and adapt them to our feelings about ourselves and other people.

Few of us act and react *exactly the same* as our parents. Times change, and public attitudes change, but basic concepts remain—perhaps altered somewhat, but essentially the same. With this modification of our values comes the realization that, with maturity, we must become *our own person.*

When we were children, our parents helped us make some of the tough decisions. In some cases, perhaps they even made them for us. But as we matured, we were expected to make more and more of our own decisions and assume more and more of the responsibility for whatever actions resulted.

Instead of expecting someone else to lead the way, we must take the initiative to achieve our own goals. Accepting that challenge will determine how "successful" we will become overall.

Several years ago, I had as a client Dr. John Kapoor, the

CEO of Lyphomed, a producer of injectable medications sold primarily to hospitals. Purchased for $4 million, it was sold eight years later, and Kapoor's stock was valued at $130 million. Kapoor and his executives got their company on the fast track and kept it there because of his basic belief in relentless pursuit and in sharing the load. His advice, "If you put your mind to something, you can achieve it. If you hit a snag, use it as a learning experience, but never attempt to do everything yourself. You can't." That's good counsel, whatever the field, whenever the time.

A Formula That Fits Every Need

Have we oversimplified a bit? Maybe. Surely some desires are more difficult to attain than others. Some people demand more of themselves than others. Some are better qualified to reach lofty goals than others.

Our targets inevitably will change from time to time. Indeed, happiness and success are moving targets.

As we age, as family and career obligations increase, as we assume greater responsibilities, our ambitions change accordingly. Yet the pathway to success and happiness tends to follow the core values that were set before we became mature adults.

Granting each individual the right to define success in his or her own terms allows each of us *to seek fulfillment in our own way*. It means that people do not have to group together in lockstep, all striving to reach the same goal. It means we can be independent, self-motivated, creative, productive, secure, and happy with our chosen lifestyles.

Top Car Seller Works at Home

At first glance, Patti Schnecke's day begins like that of any other stay-at-home mom. She gets her five kids, ages one through seven, up at 7:00 A.M. and, after getting them all clothed and fed, sees that the older ones get off to school. But by 9:00 A.M. her schedule becomes very different. That's when she gets busy answering e-mail messages at her home in Plainfield, Illinois, about forty miles southwest of Chicago.

Schnecke uses the Internet to sell cars and trucks for a Dodge Dealer in Naperville, Illinois, about fifteen miles away. And she's *very* good at it. In fact, she's the top salesperson, moving thirty vehicles a month. She goes to the dealership only to deliver vehicles and attend meetings.

Her first selling experience was in her family's restaurant, where she learned the basics of customer service. She also worked in fleet sales for other car dealers, but after seven years as a homemaker she decided to try the Internet.

Now with the help of a nanny for the children, she can respond to twenty e-mail messages a day, and she handles three hundred leads a month to net thirty sales.

Lesson: Here is a person who has achieved career momentum while at the same time getting the irreplaceable satisfactions involved in being with her children each day.

Dreams do not come in "one size fits all." We must find our own dream. Each of us must define precisely who we are, what we value in life, and how hard we are willing to work to attain success and happiness as we perceive it.

Positive Thinking Isn't Enough

Some years ago, a popular song proclaimed: "Wishing will make it so." It had a catchy melody, but the message was faulty. Wishing never made *anything* so.

As children, we wished on a star.

> Star light, star bright
> First star I've seen tonight.
> Wish I may, wish I might
> Get the wish I wish tonight.

Childhood tales of Tooth Fairies, four-leaf clovers, and enchanted forests were fascinating, but purely fanciful. Much more accurate is the adage "If wishes were horses, beggars would ride."

The secret of success is constancy of purpose.—Benjamin Disraeli

Little is ever accomplished by those who think they *cannot*. An extremely popular book titled "The Power of Positive Thinking" was produced in 1952 by Norman Vincent Peale. In it, Peale extols the value of maintaining a positive mental attitude. But "keeping good thoughts" is only one small element of the mindset that is required to be successful. Having a positive mindset, while very important, will not necessarily move you forward. It just keeps you in the game.

Wayne Huizenga, chairman of Republic Industries, Inc., believes that "Opportunities are all around us, but if you want to accomplish twice as much as your competition, *you must work twice as hard.*"

Huizenga is a well-qualified observer. Before joining Republic Industries, he was chairman of Blockbuster, Inc., and co-founder of Waste Management, Inc.

Another well-qualified observer is Jack Canfield, co-creator of the highly successful *Chicken Soup for the Soul* series of books. As an entrepreneur, Canfield had no pre-established corporate chain of command to guide him; he was entirely on his own. He, too, says that striving for success is like climbing a mountain.

"You start climbing," says Canfield, "and you hit obstacles. You have to reach inside and also look for outside support. Then, suddenly, you reach the top. You get the money—and that's nice—but what's important is *knowing that you did it.*"

> **If success doesn't come today, go on tomorrow without it.**

A good job headed by poor leaders isn't such a good job after all. Professor John Sullivan of San Francisco State University recommends five things to look for when seeking a job:

1. Be sure the job reflects your interests in life.
2. Try to find a job in which you will have a good mentor.
3. Try to find a job in which you will be able to learn a lot and learn it fast.
4. Be sure the job encourages rapid change.
5. Look for either an EOC or a FPW. (Sullivan defines an EOC as an Employer of Choice and a FPW as a Fun Place to Work. Sometimes the two will overlap.)

Money is important, of course, but so are future opportunities. Look at it this way: Would you rather take a dead-end or slow-moving job that offers you $50,000 a year or a job that offers only $40,000 a year to start but complies with Sullivan's five points? In taking Job #1, it is quite likely that you will still be making $50,000 a year five years from now. In taking Job #2, you will receive a lower salary at the outset, but it is quite possible that you could be making twice that amount within five years.

Why Good People Burn Out

But hard work does have a down side. Personal activities often must take a back seat to the demands of the job.

Employees in a company that is slow to accept change will tire out long before those who work for more progressive companies. Why? Because they must spend so much extra time and effort overcoming resistance within their own organization.

> *There's no fool like an old fool. You can't beat experience.*

The best way to prevent burnout is to simplify your life. Author Elaine St. James offers some suggestions for doing just that:

1. If you belong to any organizations whose meetings you dread attending, resign from them.
2. Stop watching the news on TV and cancel half of your magazine subscriptions. Learn to live with less information.

3. Cut your commute time. Either work where you live or live where you work.
4. Go to bed early at least one night a week.
5. Live on half of your income and save the other half.

St. James has other suggestions as well. In fact, she has created four books that are chock full of them, starting with *Simplify Your Life: 100 Ways to Slow Down and Enjoy the Things That Really Matter.* The point is that you can relieve a lot of the tension in your life if you will abandon "busywork."

If an outside activity is beneficial to you personally, or to your work, consider it. If not, graciously turn it down. Learn to prioritize your activities, reserving your energies for those that are most beneficial to *your* agenda. Conserve your time and effort. Focus on those things that are most important to you.

Winners Build—Losers Blame

Rich Melman, cofounder and CEO of Lettuce Entertain You Enterprises, Inc., credits his success to "paranoia."

"I never feel I'm good enough," says Melman. "I'm always striving to be better. I don't want to be the biggest, the richest, the most well-known; my goal is just to be as good as I can be."

A surprising number of successful business leaders echo similar feelings.

One of the best examples of sharing success is Dave Thomas, founder of Wendy's International. Thomas had a hard life growing up. He was born out of wedlock, and his mother put him up for adoption when he was six weeks old. His adoptive mother died when he was five. Struggling to make a living, his adoptive father took him from state to state, and he attended twelve different schools in just ten years.

At fifteen, Thomas was on his own. He rented a room in the Fort Wayne, Indiana, YMCA, going to school during the day and working at a Hobby House restaurant at night. Unable to handle both tasks, he dropped out of school after finishing the tenth grade and began to learn the restaurant business. In 1969, he started Wendy's.

"Mature responsibility means realizing that no one person can be responsible for everything," says Thomas. "You can't be successful if you are stumbling around, juggling the whole world on your shoulders. Responsible people take tough stands against shortcuts and have their antennae up all the time because they know the temptation to take an 'easy street' shortcut is always available."

At the age of sixty, Thomas hired a tutor and spent three months preparing to finish his high school education. He subsequently passed his GED (General Equivalency Diploma) exam, graduated with a high school class in Coconut Creek, Florida, attended the senior prom, and was voted "Most Likely to Succeed" by his fellow graduates.

Today, Thomas offers himself as an example to underprivileged children. When he is on the road, he takes the time to visit children in foster homes, in high schools, and in colleges. He stresses the importance of getting an education.

Serving as the TV spokesman for Wendy's, Thomas has made over six hundred television commercials, donating all of the fees to children's causes. "But writing a check is not enough," Thomas has been quoted as saying. "You have to let people know that you are putting money where your heart is by giving your time, too."

Like Thomas, many of the most successful people in America have endured a number of hardships along the way. They have repeatedly faced their challenges and worked to overcome them. They are justly proud of what they have been able to accomplish, while countless others look at their success, envy their achievements, and look for something—or somebody—to blame for their misfortune.

CHAPTER 3

Easy Doesn't Do It

Lou Holtz, the legendary former football coach at Notre Dame for many years, echoes the lessons learned by Wendy's Dave Thomas during his career.

"I don't care if you're running a back or coaching a football team, there isn't anyone who hasn't had to overcome something on his way to success," Holtz has said. "If you want to win, you have to get off the ground."

No Silver Bullets (The Lone Ranger Took Them All)

Lou Holtz knows what he is talking about. To win football games, a team has to set its sights on the opponent's goal line, put forth a plan, work together, and drive down the field, inch by inch and yard by yard until it crosses the goal line and scores. The team that can do it most efficiently and most often is going to win. The other team, no matter how many stars it may have on its roster or how hard it has tried, will go down in defeat.

"Winning is never accidental," adds Holtz. "All successful coaches and players have at least one thing in common: a strong game plan. I have seen teams short on talent win famous victories simply because they were better prepared and more focused on their opposition. They had clearly defined goals and consistent work habits. And they weren't afraid to make the sacrifices required to raise their play to another level. Life should be enjoyed, not feared. Fun, not work. Played, not endured. A reward, rather than a punishment."

There are no magic formulas in life, no shortcuts to success, no easy ways to get ahead. If you want to succeed in the long run, hard work, dedication, and persistence are absolute necessities. The sooner you realize that, the sooner you can start to advance.

Masaru Ibuka and Akio Morita failed in business ventures several times in post-World War II Japan. Their automatic rice cooker burned the rice, and they sold only one hundred units. Ibuka failed Toshiba's employment exam. Despondent and out of money, they built an inexpensive tape recorder and sold a few to Japanese schools. From that humble beginning, the Sony Corporation got started.

Too often, people tend to rate success in financial terms. "We need to measure our success in terms of how we treat other people," argues James Rieley, director of the Center for Continuous Quality Improvement. "Heroes are those who help us learn about how not just to 'put out fires,' but how to create environments in which we don't have those fires to contend with. Our principles and values need to guide our work lives, just as they guide our personal lives."

The late Ray Kroc, founder of McDonald's, once pointed out that nothing in the world can take the place of persistence.

"Talent will not; nothing is more common than unsuccessful men with talent," explained Kroc. "Genius will not; unrewarded genius is almost a proverb. Education alone will not; the world is full of educated derelicts. Persistence and determination alone are omnipotent."

Success Secret

There is very
little traffic,
after you begin
the extra mile.

Make Yourself Needed

President Herbert Hoover once said, "We are in danger of developing a cult of the Common Man, which means a cult of mediocrity. But there is one hopeful sign: I have never found out who this Common Man is."

"Great advances," he said "are brought about by distinctly *uncommon* people. It is a curious fact that when you get sick, you want an uncommon doctor; if your car breaks down, you want an uncommonly good mechanic. You want your children to grow up to be uncommon men and women. May it always be so. For the future rests not in mediocrity, but in the constant renewal of leadership."

In other words: Be aware of the times, which are constantly changing. Know when to act and when to bide your time. Be prepared to move when the time is right.

By refusing to recognize changes in the watch-making industry, Switzerland lost control of the watch business to Japan.

By refusing to recognize the growing impact of automobiles and airplanes, railroads lost a great deal of their once-dominant business.

Get Up—Move On

> *Talk is cheap. Don't tell people what you're going to do for them—DO IT!*

Caution is commendable, but it is not an excuse to do nothing. Quite the contrary. It is an admonition to do *something* . . . but to do it carefully.

Here are five ways to motivate yourself to move on:

1. Don't try to change everything and everyone around you.
2. Take away something good from every bad thing that happens to you.
3. Pause to appreciate the things you can't control—good weather, praise from a friend, a family member's sacrifices for you.
4. Show thanks for good health by helping someone who is sick.
5. Concentrate on gradual improvement as sensational victories.

> *A wise man will make more opportunities than he finds.*
> —*Francis Bacon*

Anne Sweeney, president of the Disney Channel in Burbank, California, is very pragmatic when it comes to evaluating opportunities and solving problems. Her usual pattern is to make detailed lists of the positives and the negatives before she makes a decision. But when the opportunity to head the Disney Channel was first offered to her, Sweeney asked herself just one question: "Will this job make my heart sing?" Under Sweeney's direction, the Disney Channel is one of the fastest-growing networks in cable television and now has more than thirty-five million subscribers.

Do not expect to sail through your career without making mistakes. Mistakes are inevitable. The secret is to learn from them and to avoid making the same mistake a second or third time.

Do not be too harsh on associates who make mistakes. Instead of criticizing them or denouncing them, help them correct their mistakes and learn from them. Next time, it may you who needs a little compassion and assistance.

> *God grant me patience . . .*
> *right now!*

Don't expect too much to happen quickly. Success usually comes at the end of the journey, not at some designated point along the road.

A number of years ago, while riding in a Chicago taxi, I found myself engaged in an interesting conversation with the driver. A few days later, there was an article about that driver in the newspaper, and I learned that he had once served as the Governor of West Virginia! Was that man a success or a failure? How, and at what point in his life, had he changed from one to the other?

Failure or Mismatch?

Michael Moritz, a general partner in Sequoia Capital in Menlo Park, California, has a one-sentence credo: "Success comes from always worrying that you're going to lose." The lesson is: If you become too confident, too complacent, something can always go wrong. Only by remaining forever vigilant can you safeguard your success.

This does not mean living in constant fear or rejecting opportunities as being too risky. Rather, we should do the things that have made us successful in the first place. The world does not stop turning and changing.

> *When you consider those who have what you believe you want, ask first, Are they truly happy?*

Make Your Own Path

Al Ueltschi is living testimony that to be successful you have to take care of your responsibilities. For as long as he can remember, he wanted to fly airplanes. He dreamed about flying during the long days he carried out his duties on the family dairy farm in Kentucky. After getting up at 4:00 A.M. and completing his chores, he earned a nickel a quart for delivering milk to people's homes.

As a teenager, he opened a hamburger shop and used the income to pay for flying lessons. Not long after that, he borrowed $3,500 to buy his own airplane. Twelve years later, he was a Pan Am pilot. Ten years after that, he started his own business. Today he is CEO of Flight Safety International, the largest pilot training company in the world.

> *Never try to teach a pig to sing.*
> *It wastes your time and it annoys*
> *the pig.* —*Paul Dickson*

Write Your Own Epitaph—I Dare You!

Admiral Mack Gaston, USN (retired), the first black commandant of the Great Lakes Naval Station, clearly recalls his father's advice: "I'm not going to tell you what you can and cannot do. I'm going to tell you what you *should* and *should not* do. How you live is *your* responsibility—not mine or your mother's. Not anyone else's but *yours*. And you don't have to worry about answering to me or to your boss, ultimately, you must answer to God. Just be sure you can face *Him*."

> *In the wide arena of the world, failure and success are not accidents as we so frequently suppose, but the strictest justice.* —*Alexander Smith*

History is not just for historians. **You are your own historian. What does your history tell you about yourself?** Your strengths? Your weaknesses? Your accomplishments? Your potential?

What does your history tell you about your relationships with other people? How will you treat them? What will you expect from them?

What does it tell you about what you value? About your priorities? About how and where you spend your time?

Above all, what does your history tell you about what you are liable to become?

The Ultimate Compliment

- From an employee or staff member: "I hope whoever follows you will be just like you."
- From a friend: "I want my children to follow your example."
- From a son or daughter to mom or dad: "I'm going to look for a husband/wife just like you."
- From a mother or father to a son or daughter: "You're just what I hoped you would be."

CHAPTER 4

A Reverence for Work

Why Work?

If reverence is defined as "honor or respect, felt or shown," how does it apply to work? First we must ask, Why do we work? Why doesn't everyone fall victim to the siren call of the politicians who promise government welfare programs?

Many certainly do. But most others (thank God they are still a majority) work to support themselves in terms of basic needs for food, clothing, and shelter.

But there is another undeniable reason. Think about it. We also work to gain the respect and admiration of those who love us. That incentive is the "gravity pull" for individuals and families. Even in tribal cultures, males and females both took pride in their respective contributions. Without the satisfactions that needed work brings, we tend to revert to today's urban gangs, for whom neither work nor life itself holds much value or meaning.

Robert Johnson's first job paid $1 per hour at a car wash in his hometown of Freeport, Illinois. He was sixteen. He learned that the best way to prevent being fired was to know every job and to do it better than the other kids. Sixteen years later, he started his own business, and, sure enough, he had to do every job himself, including advertising, marketing, preparing contracts. He strongly believes that young people who turn down low-paying jobs are only hurting themselves in the long run. He should know. He's founder, chairman, and CEO of BET Holding, Inc., which includes Black Entertainment Television, one of the largest black-owned businesses in the United States.

I strongly believe that people who do not have a reverence for work, who do not honor it or at least respect it, also do not have a true appreciation for the things that working affords them. In addition to paying for basic physical needs, work offers opportunity and the challenge to apply capabilities to their fullest.

Besides providing a paycheck and benefits, **work gives individuals a confirmation of who they are and what they can do.** Every adult who does not want to be dependent needs this confirmation continuously.

Developing a reverence for work does not mean taking the easy way out. It means making a lifelong commitment to:

Learning—The answers to today's problems will not solve the problems of tomorrow. What did today's senior citizens learn in school about computers, cellular phones, jet travel, microwave ovens, television?

Helping—Look for people who can help you, and always be prepared to repay that debt by helping others who need you.

Objectivity versus Subjectivity—If you can't measure it, you can't control it. If you can't control it, it may control you.

Perseverance—Only those who are in the game when the final whistle blows can win.

Performance—Reliable performance, day after day, leads to advancement. Every employer looks for people who get results, not those who put things off, make excuses, or rationalize failures.

To become successful, an individual needs to demonstrate a *white-hot desire* to get ahead. Being lukewarm about your work makes you average, and average doesn't equate with success.

Some individuals procrastinate, waiting for the moment when they will feel "motivated." Motivation does not strike you without warning, like the flu bug. Even getting out of bed, getting dressed, and driving to work require motivation. Motivation is something that needs to be applied to each and every task, large or small, and it almost always *follows*, rather than precedes, action.

Setting goals can be critical to formulating a successful career. Goals provide motivation and tend to keep you on track. Like having a road map, they help you reach your destination without meandering all over the countryside as you search for it.

Attaining success is seldom a sprint. It's usually a marathon. The victorious competitor will have made a total commitment to reaching the goal line through sheer persistence . . . by recognizing and overcoming any and all obstacles that may appear along the way . . . by setting his mind on victory and not even *thinking* about failure.

Joseph Hankin, president of Westchester Community College, thinks we are all rich. "If I told you," he says, "that you had $86,400 deposited to your checking account every day and that you could spend all of it every day for anything you wanted, interest-free, no repayments to make, and the next day a new $86,400 would be deposited, and every day on and on for the rest of your life, what would you think? In a way, each and every one of us does have such an account. Every morning we all have 86,400 seconds of our lives to live as we choose. We can sleep or eat them away, work, play, watch TV, hang out, or just waste them away. Success depends upon using time wisely. Time is worth more than money, and by killing time, we are killing our own chances for success."

Form a vision of what *should* be, then inspire others to help you pursue that vision. After you have modeled the way for others to follow, enable them to act so that they can help you attain that vision. When they succeed, offer them further encouragement to keep them motivated and to propel them even farther.

> *Even if you are on the right track,*
> *you'll get run over if you just sit there.*
> *—Oliver Wendell Holmes*

Maya Angelou, author of the bestseller *I Know Why the Caged Bird Sings* and a Reynold professor of American Studies at Wake Forest University, talks about a lesson she learned from her grandmother.

"When my grandmother was raising me in Stamps, Arkansas," says Angelou, "she had a particular routine when people who were known to be whiners entered her store. My grandmother would ask the customer: 'How are you doing today, Brother Thomas?' And the person would reply: 'Not so good today, Sister Henderson. You see, it's this summer heat. I just hate it. It just frazzles me up and frazzles me down. It's almost killing me.'

"As soon as the complainer was out of the store, my grandmother would call me to stand in front of her. And then she would say: 'Sister, did you hear what Brother So-and-So complained about?' And I would not.

"Mamma would continue: 'Sister, there are people who went to sleep all over the world last night, poor and rich and white and black, but they will never wake again. And those dead folks would give anything, anything at all for just five minutes of this weather that person was grumbling about. So you watch yourself about complaining. What you're supposed to do when you don't like a thing is change it. Change the way you think about it. Don't complain."

> *There is a four-letter word that describes every good thing that happens—work.*

Some failure is inevitable. Everyone we may now consider to be successful has suffered failures in the past. They regain momentum because they do not let temporary setbacks destroy their commitment or their resolve. Instead, they set aside their disappointment, regroup, and move on with even better results. To regain control:

1. Get rid of the blame.
2. Stop being a victim
3. Get a family member or friend to give you moral and emotional support while you work your way out of the situation.

4. Set your priorities.
5. Create a plan for the future.
6. Set deadlines for each action you will take.

Is a College Degree the Answer?

Too many people consider themselves limited because they did not graduate from college. Whatever the reason, that fact should not be used as an excuse for lack of accomplishment.

Forbes magazine recently conducted a survey of the four hundred wealthiest Americans. They learned that fifty-eight (14.5 percent) of those high achievers either avoided college completely or dropped out before graduation. Indeed, while the average net worth of the *Forbes* four hundred is $1.8 billion, that of the fifty-eight individuals who did *not* graduate from college is $4.8 billion—167 percent higher!

True, the average college graduate earns $40,000 a year, according to another study, while the average high school graduate earns just a little more than half that amount—$22,895. But these are *averages*, and they do not reflect the significant achievements of many *individuals* within the categories. Remember, to be average simply means that you are either the best of the worst or the worst of the best. In actuality, 46 percent of the college graduates working in the service sector earn less than an *average* high school graduate. So do 45 percent of the college graduates engaged in farming, transportation, machine operation, and general labor; 42 percent of the college graduates employed in administrative support; 26 percent of the college graduates engaged in retail sales; and 24 percent of the college graduates working in precision production, craft, or repair work. Obviously, a college degree is not a surefire passport to achievement.

The Busyness Trap

Christopher Higgins, senior vice president of payment services at the Bank of America in San Francisco, says he simplified his life a great deal through an easy three-step process:

Step 1—He had his project managers make a list of each of the projects they were working on. Each project was to be described in one sentence, and each project was to be written on a separate index card.

> *Only two events yield progress:*
> *thinking and work—in that order.*

Step 2—Higgins then arranged all of the index cards so that similar or related projects were grouped together.

Step 3—As he categorized the project descriptions, he noted that a number of them connected, duplicated, or overlapped one another. He then killed any duplicate projects and consolidated others wherever it seemed possible and appropriate. Was this simple? You bet!

What were the results? Higgins claims that the first time he used this technique he was able to eliminate one-third of all the projects that his staff had been working on and consolidated many others.

> *A wise old owl sat on an oak*
> *the more he saw the less he spoke;*
> *The less he spoke the more he learned;*
> *Why aren't we like that wise old bird?*
> —*Edward Hersey Richards*

The best way to avoid the "busyness" trap is to separate important issues from the insignificant ones. This means *prioritize.* Then take care of the most important matters first. Let low priorities wait.

Are You "Referenceable"?

Are you the kind of person other people quote or seek out for opinions? If so, you are "referenceable." You are seen as an authority in certain areas. People look to you for advice. They value your opinions.

To be referenceable, you must achieve a reputation for personal and professional integrity. That can best be accomplished by (a) accuracy, (b) honesty, (c) integrity, and (d) avoiding prejudgments.

These qualities are basic:

- A referenceable individual is skilled at distinguishing a perception from a fact. Why? Because action based on perception is often misdirected.
- A referenceable individual avoids polarization by shunning either-or situations. She realizes that there are a number of other possibilities *besides the two*

that can bring satisfactory resolution to what may seem to be a dilemma.

- A referenceable individual recognizes that it can be dangerous to concentrate only on perfection, because he has learned that this can make you a slave to a single answer instead of allowing you to consider other possibilities. He also realizes that it is foolish to be overzealous and lose sight of reality.
- A referenceable individual must have a stake in the organization, in its values, and in its success. He must earn the right to expect excellence from others by always striving to attain excellence himself.

> *Nothing is so embarrassing as watching someone do something that you said couldn't be done.*

- A referenceable individual must be persistent yet patient. He cannot be driven solely by the promise of some reward. Some things must be done simply because they're the right thing to do. He must give recognition to others and restrain the urge to criticize. Perhaps most important of all, he must learn to say "we" instead of "I."
- A referenceable individual must be decisive. He must get out front and lead. He must demonstrate that the *application* of knowledge and skill is far more important than being endowed with them.
- A referenceable individual values diversity. She rec-

ognizes that being persuasive is often better than seeking control. She takes issues more seriously than herself.

Leadership is situational; neither one person nor one style is the best under all circumstances.

Thinking: The Hardest Work There Is

Decision-making is more a process than an event. It begins with defining the problem clearly and then evaluating options by weighing alternatives.

> *We tend to resist wisdom.*
> *That is why we are not fond*
> *of those who make us think.*

When approaching a problem, try to think creatively. Change your outlook from negative to positive. Look for the root cause of the problem. Ask yourself if there is a preliminary problem to be resolved. Determine whether there are any minimum conditions associated with the solution. What must the solution accomplish? What elements must the solution contain? What would an ideal solution look like?

Weigh the possible solutions against an ideal situation. Then ask yourself, "What's the worst possible outcome if this decision doesn't work?"

Create ways to evaluate your decision. How can you tell if you're making progress? How will you measure success? Set a deadline and, if possible, sub-deadlines. Monitor the solution on a regular basis.

When you are ready to carry out your solution, try to develop a sense of urgency. The longer you wait to begin, the less your chance of being satisfied that you have found the right answer.

Mind Scars

Mind scars are bad experiences we won't allow to heal. They are reminders of past problems that are best forgotten. Unlike scars on the body, they continue to grow until they begin to affect many of our actions and decisions. We let them plague us, load us down with guilt, burden us with uncertainty. They have a negative impact on our outlook, our relationships, our careers, and sometimes on our entire life..

Don Yacktman, a fifty-seven-year-old investment fund manager, is a perfect example of how mind scars can kill momentum. He believes in investing in small companies, and nothing will shake him from that commitment.

By 1990, the record of his *Selected American Shares* fund had topped over 60 percent of all equity fund managers, and assets had reached $400 million. After starting his own fund in 1992, he made three decisions that his critics say began his downfall: (1) Over 70 percent of the assets became controlled by large institutional investors. (2) He hired an inexperienced member of his church as a stock analyst. (3) He hired his son, Steve, who was then twenty-three, as a stock analyst. His comment about his son is especially revealing. "There is no sense in bringing in someone you have to argue with," he said.

After enjoying a period of success in the mid 1990s, the

Yacktman Fund began to head for disaster in 1998. Yacktman was accused by three board members of having a conflict of interest with one of the companies he had invested in. His favorite small capitalization stocks were down 75 percent in 1999 after trailing the S&P 500 by 28 percent in 1998. Investors continue to abandon the man whose momentum has been stopped cold by what his enemies call "a rebellious disregard for his fund's investment mandate" and a refusal to acknowledge others' viewpoints.

Few, if any, mind scars can be hidden permanently, but they *can* be used as a learning experience *if we can only learn to keep them in perspective.* The objective is to not allow them to destroy our self-confidence.

Mind scars almost always result from things that happen to us or that we allow to happen, not from things that we *make* happen. They are often the principal causes of stress in our lives. They should be put aside or moved to the past while we concentrate on becoming successful in whatever we have elected to do with our lives.

> *You can use normal life stress to toughen yourself. Tough times represent opportunities for getting better.*
> *—James Loebr, Sports Psychologist*

CHAPTER   5

How To Be a Rainmaker

No doubt about it—General Electric is probably the most successful company of modern times. It was already one of the world's largest when Jack Welch became CEO in 1981. Now it is almost four times larger than it was then. An investor who put $10,000 into GE stock when Welch took office would have seen that investment grow to over $370,000 today—a multiple of thirty-seven times in eighteen years!

Here are the key principles that Welch lives by:

Never stop looking for ways to do your job better. Don't be afraid to go above and beyond what has been expected of you. If change is needed, be the one to suggest it. Instead of fearing change; expect it. Anticipate the ways it might affect you and your job. If you are not a part of change, it will leave you behind.

Stop managing people, and begin to lead them. Too many managers get bogged down in monitoring and supervising. They create bureaucratic sluggishness that stifles inventiveness and prevents the introduction of new ways of thinking.

Instead of "policing" the people who are responsible to you, motivate and energize them. Make them want to do their very best. Give them your vision of what can be done. Fire them up and get out of their way.

Don't focus solely on numbers. Those who look solely at the numbers aren't seeing the entire picture. They aren't considering the marketplace or the competition. They aren't thinking about new products and new services or getting needed input from the people who do the work.

When the numbers are good, it's easy to get the mistaken impression that *everything* is good when, in fact, big trouble could be looming just ahead.

> ### Winners make tools. Losers wait for others to provide tools for them.

Look for, and accept, new ideas. "No matter how gifted an individual is," Welch says, "he can't succeed on his own. He needs to look to others as a fresh source of ideas. He needs to look to customers . . . to competitors . . . to find out who's doing something exceptional, and then copy them."

Cross over barriers. Make contacts and allies everywhere you can. Try to see how you can help others and how they can help you. Barter when you can't pay cash. Let people know that you are open to discuss their ideas. When you yourself become compartmentalized, you lose your momentum.

Excessive attention to numbers alone is well illustrated by the decline of Addressograph-Multigraph Corporation.

A-M had two products on the market that seemed totally irreplaceable: the Addressograph labeling system and the Multigraph offset duplicator.

The Addressograph used small metal plates onto which various types of information were impressed—typically a customer's name and address. The plates were widely used to implement mass mailings, and literally millions of them were used by American businesses every year. Magazines used them to address their subscribers. Direct-mail advertisers used them the same way. During wartime, the GI "dog tag" was simply an Addressograph plate hanging from a neck chain.

A-M's other seemingly irreplaceable product, the Multilith offset duplicator, was an inexpensive means of reproducing reports, newsletters, advertising flyers, and similar materials. The machines came in various sizes, but in simple terms, they were small, inexpensive, easy-to-operate printing presses.

Lulled into overconfidence because "the numbers were good," A-M's management became entrenched and complacent. The company allowed itself to grow top-heavy with highly paid executives who had little to do. Research and development was virtually nonexistent. Nobody paid attention to two new products that suddenly came onto the market: the photocopier and the computer.

Typically, when a company set up a Multilith operation, it was housed in an out-of-the-way area stocked with such necessary accessories as paper, ink, and cleaning equipment. If an executive needed several copies of a document, he typically sent a memo to the Multilith department, requesting them to do it. The job might be delivered by an in-house messenger a day or two later. By contrast, the photocopier could do everything that the Multilith did . . . and more. It was cheaper, smaller, cleaner, more flexible, and easier to operate, and it fit nicely into a business office, where anyone who needed to use it could have ready access to it.

Much like the Multilith, the Addressograph was generally housed in a large, out-of-the-way area and required a good deal of space to store the new and used plates. Even more, the machines required a dedicated staff to operate them. Businesses soon learned that the computer could maintain mailing lists much more quickly, easily, and less expensively. It could electronically store a much larger database and make it more readily available for other uses. In short, the computer was far more responsive than the Addressograph.

In a few short years, Addressograph-Multigraph slipped from its position as a Fortune 500 company into bankruptcy, while the manufacturers of office copiers and computers founded vast new industries that are vital to today's commerce.

Strong Bow, Empty Quiver—The Value of Being Prepared

The surest route to success is to be on the ground floor of a major introduction of a new product or the development of a new market.

The knack is to release the past and focus on the future—to visualize not how things were, but how they can be. Visionaries are not always successful, but without them progress is slow at best.

John Wooden, the phenomenal coach who took UCLA to ten NCAA basketball championships in twelve years during the 1960s and 1970s, *never attempted to have his teams copy the previous year's performance*. Instead, he asked *each* team to strive for its *own kind* of perfection. To him, it was far better to teach his players the inspirational effects of achievement than to drill into them the fear of failure.

Be Your Own Mentor

While having a mentor may be beneficial in some instances, there is even more advantage for those who prepare to be their own mentor. When you are not dependent on someone else to guide you, you are more likely to be in control of your own career.

The road to success begins when you prepare yourself to win a place on a team. Developing skills the employer needs comes before selling yourself into a job. Never stop learning. Know your values and stick with them. Think carefully about how to respond to those who challenge your ideas or values.

Reputation is built by following a few simple principles:

- **Establish achievable goals with reasonable deadlines.** If you don't know where you're going, any road will get you there.
- **Keep your promises.** If you don't think this is important, recall your feeling the last time someone lied to you.
- **Develop quality friendships around you.** These people will support you in good times and will protect you from more trouble in bad times.
- **Solve the problem closest to you.** Don't waste time on imaginary or unfixable problems.
- **Respect the good qualities in your boss.** Help over come whatever weaknesses your boss may have.

- **Protect your reputation.** Treat it as a priceless pos
  session. Recognize that every time you compromise
  it you reduce your net worth with assets you can
  never replenish.

Manipulating Minutia

Little is gained by "tilting at windmills." When we are engrossed
in details, far more important issues pass us by.

Don't let other people's minutia become your minutia. Try
these suggestions:

- **Change their outlook.** Acknowledge concerns.
  Show empathy. Be patient. Stay calm, but resolute.
- **Change the situation.** Introduce new options. "Let's
  try this and see what happens." Or "Maybe this
  would work better." Or "This worked before. Let's
  try it again."
- **Change yourself.** Back away from the situation long
  enough to ask yourself if it's worth all the attention
  that you've been giving it. If not, drop it.

One of the best ways to keep other people's minutia from
bogging you down is to drastically reduce meetings. Most meetings could be replaced by a well-written memo, fax, or e-mail to
the individual who will be the ultimate decision-maker. If that
person decides it would be useful to have additional input from
others, just get it!

> *Nothing is particularly hard if you divide it into small jobs.*—*Henry Ford*

If a presentation is absolutely necessary:

- Block out time to prepare; don't try to "wing it."
- Start with an outline, even if you plan eventually to write out the entire talk. It will keep your thoughts on track.
- Take "The Great Circle Route"—tell your audience what you plan to say, say it, and then tell them what you have said.
- Keep it simple; don't try to cover more ground than necessary. Close with a strong call to action.
- Make it a talk, not a speech. Eliminate the word "I." Be conversational. Use every-day language. Relax.
- Use visual aids whenever they will make your points easier to remember.

Don't Waste Time On Yesterday

Jim McCann, CEO of 1-800-FLOWERS, considers himself a "creative plagiarist."

"Enter every situation, every encounter, every meeting, every interview with the intention of learning something," says McCann. "Develop the ability to learn from others' experience and to apply those lessons in new situations. In almost everything new that you attempt, someone has already done it, sometimes successfully and sometimes not. There is a lesson to learn either way."

To handle new situations, you often need to acquire new skills. You need to learn how to approach an issue three-dimensionally, changing your perspective, your attitude, your objective, if necessary. Learn to simplify your life by treating mistakes as a necessary path to success.

When people make minor mistakes—and they will—let them suffer the consequences. That is part of learning. While you may want to shield them from *major* mistakes, keep in mind that it is the consequences of mistakes that yield learning . . . and eventually lead to success.

> *To thrive tomorrow,*
> *I must survive today.*

To eliminate minutia is to simplify your work day. Eliminate needless paperwork. Cut expenses. Toss old files. Store little-used information on disks. Prioritize all correspondence, phone calls, faxes, and e-mail. Don't worry about offending those at the bottom of the priority list.

> *Knowing makes the start.*
> *Doing makes the difference.*

The best way to keep a business moving ahead is to continually search for and hire good people. Find people who have no trouble telling it like it is. Find ways to let employees tell how well they think their bosses are doing their job.

There's nothing like seeing how your opinion of your performance differs from your boss's opinion.

Excellent Excuses

As luck would have it, Jim McCann encountered Jack Welch, CEO of General Electric, at a dinner party one evening.

"I had to fire a senior person in the company," says McCann. "Everyone knew he wasn't right for the job. Everyone knew I wasn't dealing with the problem. But this guy was a friend.

"It's never easy to fire someone, but in this case, it was brutal."

At the dinner party, McCann discussed the situation with Jack Welch.

"When was the last time anyone said, 'I wish I had waited six months longer to fire that guy?'" asked Welch. "Always err on the side of speed."

Welch's advice motivated McCann to deal with the situation a few days later.

"It hurt—but I felt such relief," says McCann. "The pain soon went away, and now my friendship with my former colleague is back on track. It was the right decision for everyone."

McCann stopped making excuses and got the job done.

We have all heard the most common excuses for below par performance: "I can't." "I didn't have the time." "You didn't tell me." "You didn't show me." "You didn't ask me."

Excuses are an excellent measure of ambition. The more frequent the excuses, the lower the true ambition.

Michael Wheeler, professor of Management in the Harvard

Business School, hits the nail on the head: "The more you avoid the truth, the steeper the price you are likely to pay in terms of wasted effort and frustration."

Listen to these current examples from top executives.

Jerry Hirshberg, president of Nissan Design International, Inc., of San Diego, California, uncovers the awful truth about meetings: "Many of the best ideas are communicated through whispers—in the hallway meetings that happen after the official meeting," he says. "That's because people worry about how the boss will react if they speak the truth. What's remarkable is that these whispered ideas are what companies say they are most hungry for."

Remember: Winners never bat 1,000.

Robert Rodin, president and CEO of Marshall Industries in El Monte, California, says: "The more you insist on hearing the truth, and the more often you act on what you've heard, the more often people will give it to you. At least once a month, I convene a forum [at which] I gather people at one of our sites; no managers are allowed. I start every meeting by saying something like: 'This is your company. Tell me what's wrong with it.'

"We don't always do what people want; companies aren't democracies. But people know that we haven't just heard their criticisms; we've dealt with them."

Katherine Hudson, president and CEO of the W. H. Brady Company in Milwaukee, Wisconsin, tells an amusing anecdote about her father, who "told me everything that I know about taking risks."

When her father graduated from high school, he couldn't afford to go to college, so he became a messenger boy at Eastman Kodak. His duties included running notes up and down the company's nineteen-story office tower and cleaning and refilling the inkwells in the executive offices.

One day the young man's boss said, "Ed, can you type?" To which Hudson's father immediately replied "Yes!"—even though he had never touched a typewriter in his life. That evening, Ed borrowed his sister's typewriter and began to teach himself how to type. He couldn't learn everything in one weekend, so he decided to concentrate solely on learning the letters. On Monday morning, he was assigned to his new duties in Kodak's billing department, typing numbers.

Later Katherine also went to work for Kodak, where she stayed for twenty-four years and became the firm's top female executive. Early in her career there, she was required to write a report explaining the company's new and complicated reorganization process. At the end of the day, her boss asked her what she thought of the reorganization. She said she thought it was a good idea, but that she felt sorry for the poor guy who had to run the instant-photography division—a unit that had been losing several million dollars a year. "Well, how would you like to be that poor guy?" her boss inquired. Hudson accepted the challenge, put together a management team, and turned the division around in fifteen months.

Today Hudson can reflect back on what her father had taught

her, and she can say, "I wasn't going to let fear or doubt keep me from saying, 'Yes, I can type.'"

Information—Power or Burden?

Debra Speight, vice president of Information Technology and CIO of Harvard Pilgrim Health Care in Lexington, Massachusetts, advises, "The real challenge is not *whether* to tell the truth but *when*. We process so much information so fast that it's easy to hear only what you want to hear.

"If I've learned anything about candor in business, it's that timing is everything. Even if you don't have a problem with telling the truth, the person on the receiving end of the conversation might have a problem with hearing it. So on those rare occasions when you have someone's undivided attention, be direct and honest."

> *Denial is not a river in Egypt.*

Jack Stack, president and CEO of SRC Holdings Corporation in Springfield, Missouri, has a good reason to avoid making excuses.

"The more people understand what's really going on in the company, the more eager they are to help solve its problems," says Stack. "Information isn't power; it's a burden. Share information and you share the burdens of leadership as well."

Don't Build Fences For Your Mind

People often can be their own worst enemy.

Scott Adams, a cartoonist with United Feature Syndicate in New York, tells about a time he was paired up in tennis with a woman who was just learning the game.

"Every time she missed a shot, she immediately turned to me, expecting that I would be disappointed or frustrated," says Adams. "Instead, I talked to her about our strategy for the next point. By doing so, I sent a very clear signal: The past doesn't matter.

"I didn't encourage her with empty praise—that approach rarely works. But I knew that if she dwelled on a mistake, she was more likely to repeat it, and that if she focused on how we were going to win the next point, she was more likely to help us do just that."

Ross West, president of Difference Communications in Rome, Georgia, believes that people can be happier in their work by following a few simple suggestions:

1. Be thankful your work helps you.
2. Be glad your work helps others.
3. Be thankful for activities besides work.

> *Work is the rent you pay for the room you occupy on earth. —Elizabeth, the Queen Mother*

Attitude Makes the Difference

Attitude plays a major role in your attempts to succeed and in your chances of attaining happiness. *Choose* to succeed; *refuse* to fail. Commit yourself to becoming successful, and you are likely to have the courage to get it done. Develop confidence in yourself, but don't expect too much. To refuse to admit failure is blind ambition.

Develop the characteristics that lead to success: Believability. Trustworthiness.

See the mission, the project, and the people you're working with as bigger than yourself, and you may develop charisma—the ability to inspire others.

Jay Conger, who is with the University of Southern California business school, created a simple little do-it-yourself quiz to determine your "charisma quotient":

1. I worry most about
   a) my current competitors
   b) my future competitors
2. I'm most at ease thinking in
   a) generalities
   b) specifics
3. I tend to focus on
   a) our missed opportunities
   b) opportunities we've seized
4. I prefer to
   a) promote traditions that made us great
   b) create new traditions
5. I like to communicate an idea via
   a) a written report
   b) a one-page chart

6. I tend to ask
    a) "How can we do this better?"
    b) "Why are we doing this?"
7. I believe
    a) there's always a way to minimize risk
    b) some risks are too high
8. When I disagree with my boss, I typically
    a) coax him nicely to alter his view
    b) bluntly tell him, "You're wrong."
9. I tend to swap people by using
    a) emotion
    b) logic
10. I think this quiz is
    a) ridiculous
    b) fascinating

ANSWERS: 1. b; 2. a; 3. a; 4. b; 5. b; 6. b; 7. a; 8. b; 9. a; 10. b.

According to Conger, if you made the correct choice on four or fewer of the questions, you probably don't have much charisma. If you answered correctly on seven or more questions, you're oozing with it.

Listen to what you are saying, because we tend to *become* what we *think*. Rainmakers tend to become what they think they can be. They prompt themselves.

Who Is Your Prompter? (It Better Be You!)

We all need a little shove from time to time. The question is— how often? Who shoves you? Your boss? A friend? Your parents?

Your spouse? If you're a rainmaker, you have learned to shove *yourself.*

- Visualize where you want to be a month, a year, and five years down the line.
- Keep a journal of your progress.
- Don't indulge in self-pity.
- Affirm yourself every time you get the chance.
- Behave like the person you wish to become.

Don't delay. Remove worrisome mind blocks by reminding yourself of your successes, time after time, over and over. Build on them. Remember that **confidence grows with achievement.**

CHAPTER 6

The Power of Persistence

Persistence separates good intentions from results. It is the key to determining whether dreams will ever become reality. The power of persistence depends upon an understanding and application of a number of commitments:

1. Are you willing to constantly push yourself to do more?
2. Can you be objective about yourself? Do you know your weaknesses and work to overcome them?
3. Do you look for what's wrong before finding someone to blame?
4. Do you study to see why when good things happen?
5. Do you set clear performance standards for your self *before* you tell others what you expect from them?
6. Do you insist that those who create problems are responsible for finding solutions?

7. Do you change policies that stifle accountability?
8. Do you avoid over-directing, over-reporting and over-managing?
9. Do you know how to create a climate in which people will be self-motivated? Have you done it?
10. Can you sustain yourself over time with little praise or credit?

It's Better to Avoid Dragons Than to Slay Them

Somebody is upset—and blaming you. What can you do?

- First, don't make excuses. They just provide more fuel for the fire.
- Next, don't get angry. If you flare up, it will only make matters worse. Instead, keep your voice at its usual level and slow down both your speech and your body motions. Be calm. Choose your words carefully. Don't overreact.
- Suggest that you sit down somewhere and discuss the issue quietly. Ask for more information.
- Avoid loaded language such as "What a dumb thing to say." "That's a lie." "You don't know what you're talking about."
- Don't interrupt. Attempt to find a mutually acceptable solution to the problem.
- Ask, "What will make you happy?" Then ask, "If I give you that will you give me this?"
- Keep in mind that the goal is not always winning, but sometimes finding a solution you can live with.

Excuse-makers don't like to keep score.

Rather than make excuses, it is far more productive to do some soul-searching to discover *why* you failed to do whatever was expected.

- Did you lack the necessary resources? Should you have asked for an extension of time, more people to work with you, more money? Whatever the reason, if you had communicated the need for additional resources early on, there would be no need to offer excuses now.
- Did you get proper instructions? If not, why not?

One lie or "cover up" can haunt you forever.

When you make excuses, you are really trying to absolve yourself of responsibility. You are attempting to place the blame for your lack of achievement on something or someone other than yourself. Unless you break that habit, your ultimate excuse will be, "Nothing good ever happens to me, but I can't help it."

Coping With Failure

The people who framed our Declaration of Independence granted us certain inalienable rights: life, liberty, and the *pursuit* of happiness. They said we had the right to *pursue* it, but nobody ever gave us any assurance that we would always be able to *capture* it.

The formula for failure is clear: Never accept responsibility.

When Naomi Judd was seventeen, she got pregnant and married her boyfriend. Five years later she found herself living two thousand miles from home with two kids to support, no husband, and no job. Without a car, she found a minimum-wage job as a receptionist within walking distance of her apartment. She did things no one else wanted to do and was soon promoted. She quickly learned she was more capable than she thought she was, and she has proven it many times since. This is the same Naomi Judd who has won six Grammy Awards and sold over twenty million country music albums.

When Netscape Communications suffered severe financial losses in 1998 and was forced to lay off 10 percent of its employees, Rich Coulter, then the director of intranet-server development at the company, began to formulate an exit plan. Today, Coulter is a vice president at Pocket Science, Inc., in Santa Clara, California.

> *Push away worry with work.*

Failure doesn't result from the lack of achievement; it comes from the lack of *trying*.

This is not to say that the pathway to success is without its hazards. Disillusionment lurks around every corner. But those who aspire to success must learn how to face it, how to deal with it, and how to go on with the more positive aspects of their careers.

It helps to learn the difference between a setback and a failure. Failure is destructive. A setback can be overcome . . . can be instructive . . . can be constructive . . . can be character-building.

People who suffer a setback, pick themselves up, regroup, and try again. Those who experience failure simply give up.

The trick to gaining momentum is to overcome the feeling of loss as quickly as possible and replace it with a positive experience. Even if it is a minor victory, it will set the stage for you to reach new heights.

> *Winners are perceptive,*
> *positive and persistent.*

Success is the result of a career based upon accomplishment. Accomplishment is the result of developing a talent for making good decisions.

Ed Koch, former mayor of New York City and now a media personality, says you must have confidence in yourself to make good decisions.

"As the mayor of New York for twelve years, I had a $28 billion budget," says Koch. "Each decision I made affected seven and a half million people. The stakes were high, so I had to show confidence—in particular, confidence in my decision-making ability—because a lot of people had put their trust in me."

But Koch admits that he had made his share of bad decisions, too.

"The worst decision I ever made was to run for governor of New York State in 1982," he says. "I did it on a lark, and it was stupid. Thank God the people of New York had enough sense to understand that I didn't have my heart in that race—and to vote against me. They did the right thing . . . and I was happier because of it."

"We all make bad decisions," says Koch. "The important thing is not to worry too much about them. Otherwise, you'll never do a thing."

> ### *Apathy can be as dangerous as ignorance.*

Making sound business decisions is not unlike making sound personal decisions. Good decisions depend on answers to two questions:

- What are my skills?
- What should I be doing *now* to get where I want to be *later?*

"Forget it kid, you'll never make it." That's what they told Jamie Moyer. You see, he is only 5'8" and weights 145 pounds. Yet he's been a big-league baseball pitcher for the past fifteen years. The little guy has been released six times and traded three times. But he has found the fast track and is now better than ever. For the past three years, he has had the best winning percentage of any pitcher in the major leagues!

Amazingly, Moyer has gained his momentum and kept his

career alive without a fastball. He can't overpower anyone, so he taught himself control. He consistently puts the ball where he wants it to go. He outsmarts hitters with a variety of off-speed pitches designed to get batters to hit the ball on the ground, where his teammates can handle it.

His advice: The *only* way to consistently hit a target is to practice.

As Senior Director of Officiating for the National Football League, Jerry Seeman knows what it's like to make a lot of decisions. And in his case, it generally takes but a few seconds to learn whether you've made the right one or the wrong one. The players, the coaches, and the fans are quick to give you their decision.

Seeman's key to making good decisions?

"You must be in position, you must have a deep knowledge of the game, and you must have intense concentration," he says. "No matter what the reaction to your decision may be, you answer to only one thing: your conscience."

Put into business parlance, the "secret" of making good decisions would follow Seeman's example precisely. Get into position, know "the rules of the game," and concentrate.

> *Security is portable. If you can't take it with you, you really don't have it.*

The Fine Art of Hunkering

Sometimes the best strategy is one I call "hunkering." It means that in some tough situations the best thing you can do is simply "hunker down" and wait for the storm to blow over.

Making hasty decisions under such circumstances can be dangerous. So why not wait until you're in a better position to study alternatives more fully and evaluate a clear course of action?

Kirby Dyess, Vice President and Director of New Business Development for Intel Corporation believes she can tell when she needs to readjust her life. The three clues are when she loses empathy, when she becomes frustrated with interruptions, or when she hears her young daughter say, "It'll be okay mom."

To get back on track she takes time out and looks for ways to simplify her life. She doesn't work harder, but she does something she finds relaxing and enjoyable, like gardening. She also gives people permission to get away from work awhile when she spots obvious signs of stress. More effort is not always the answer. Sometimes to "get a life" you must simply hunker down until the storm passes over.

Things Aren't Always What They Seem

Two traveling angels stopped to spend the night in the home of a wealthy family. The family was rude and refused to let the angels stay in the mansion's guest room. Instead, the angels were given a space in the cold basement. As they made their bed on the hard floor, the older angel saw a hole in the wall and repaired it. When the younger angel asked why, the older angel replied, "Things aren't always what they seem."

The next night the pair came to rest at the house of a very poor but very hospitable farmer and his wife. After sharing what little food they had, the couple let the angels sleep in their bed, where they could have a good night's rest. When the sun came up the next morning, the angels found the farmer and his wife in tears. Their only cow, whose milk had been their sole income, lay dead in the field. The younger angel was infuriated and asked the older angel, "How could you have let this happen? The first man had everything, yet you helped him," she accused. "The second family had little but was willing to share everything, and you let their cow die." "Things aren't always what they seem," the older angel replied. "When we stayed in the basement of the mansion, I noticed there was gold stored in that hole in the wall. Since the owner was so obsessed with greed and unwilling to share his good fortune, I sealed the wall so he wouldn't find it. Then last night as we slept in the farmer's bed, the angel of death came for his wife. I gave her the cow instead. Things aren't always what they seem."

Sometimes this is exactly what happens when things don't turn out the way they should. If you have faith, you just need to trust that every outcome is always to your advantage. You might not know it until sometime later—so you just have to hunker down and wait.

> *The side roads are filled with brainy people who started fast, but ran out of gas. They were replaced by slower, plain, deliberate types who just kept going and never looked back.*

Deborah Triant, CEO and president of Check Point Software Technologies, Inc., in Redwood City, California, believes making and implementing decisions boils down to one key ingredient: listening.

"The worst thing that a leader can do in the decision-making process," says Triant, "is to voice your opinion before anybody else can. No matter how open and honest your people are, stating your opinion first will short-change the discussion process and taint what you hear later.

"I often wonder why schools emphasize debating. Why not have *listening* classes as well?"

I wholeheartedly agree. Let's start a citizen's campaign to require that listening be taught in every school district in the land!

The Source of Power

The source of power lies in the support and performance of those who do the work. You can accomplish only so much as an individual. To be truly successful, you must form ... and then lead ... a competent, self-motivated team.

> *Success depends on three things: who says it, what he says, how he says it; and of these three things, what he says is the least important—John, Viscount Morley*

Qad's chairman and president, Pamela Lopker, expresses it this way: "As a leader, I try not to make decisions for others. Sure, being a dictator is often the fastest way to get things done, but it's not a process that allows an organization to sustain growth. I want the people in my organization to learn the lessons that come with making decisions: that everything is a compromise, and that nothing is ever completely logical."

Lopker heads one of the thirty largest public companies in America to be led by a female CEO.

Rudyard Kipling's famous poem "If" captures, I believe, the power of persistence as well as anything ever written:

> If you can keep your head when all about you
>> Are losing theirs and blaming it on you,
> If you can trust yourself when all men doubt you,
>> But make allowance for their doubting too;
> If you can wait and not be tired by waiting,
>> Or being lied about, don't deal in lies,
> Or being hated, don't give way to hating,
>> And yet don't look too good, nor talk too wise:
> If you can dream—and not make dreams your master;
>> If you can think—and not make thoughts your aim;
> If you can meet with Triumph and Disaster
>> And treat those two impostors just the same.
> If you can make one heap of all your winnings
>> And risk it on one turn of pitch-and-toss,
> And lose, and start again at your beginnings
>> And never breathe a word about your loss.
> If you can talk with crowds and keep your virtue,
>> Or walk with Kings—nor lose the common touch,
> If neither foes nor loving friends can hurt you,
>> If all men count with you, but none too much;

If you can fill the unforgiving minute
    With sixty seconds' worth of distance run,
Yours is the Earth and everything that's in it,
    And—which is more—you'll be a Man, my son!

CHAPTER 7

Living Above Fear

> *Greatness is not sought. It is the*
> *outcome of unselfish acts to benefit others.*

The real tragedy in life is not that so many people fail to succeed, but that so many refuse to try.

They drop out when they realize that they are facing strong competition, that there is no shortcut to success and no easy route to follow. If there were, we would all be multimillionaires.

Mahatma Gandhi knew how to live above fear. "I am," he said, "an average person with below-average capabilities. I have not the shadow of a doubt that any man or woman can achieve what I have if he or she would put forth the same effort and cultivate the same hope and faith."

Too many people are content to lie back and accept whatever life gives them. Often, this is because of fear—the fear of failure, the fear of exposing their shortcomings. Sometimes it's simply because they can't decide what it is that they truly want to achieve in life.

Fear is the opposite of courage. When fear controls, there is no progress.

Does a baseball player throw strikes on every pitch? Or hit home runs on every trip to the plate?

Does a golfer ace every hole? Or sink every putt?

Does a bowler throw a strike on every ball? Or, barring that, is he always successful in picking up the spare on his second try?

Does a gambler win every pot?

To win, you must be in the game, spectators simply sit by and watch. Failure is a part of life. Most people believe they learn a great deal more from their failures than they do from their successes. And that is how we should view our failures: Not just as inevitable, but as a necessary part of learning.

> *Two days in the week should never be feared: yesterday and tomorrow.*

When Will You Flinch?

The hardest work in the world is not coal mining or even running a marathon. Sure, they both require lots of physical energy, but be honest. What do you avoid? What makes you most uncomfortable? It's *thinking*, especially when there is no quick or easy solution.

Those who exercise good judgment throughout their lives actually follow a rather simple process. They carefully think through the consequences of their actions and then modify their behavior to bring about the desired result.

To think through a situation properly, you must consider the ways in which your own biases and preferences might be affecting your decisions; obtain evidence to support your views, rather than simply assume that those views are correct; and envision and investigate a range of possibilities and opportunities before taking action.

> *Thinking is the hardest work there is.*
> *That's why we tend to avoid it.*

Thinking through a situation permits you to analyze what you have been told *before* you act on it. It allows you to evaluate the impact of what you say and do.

Solid thinking comes from looking at both sides of an issue. It is not from *confirming* your biases, but *challenging* them. It is based on open-minded, but not gullible, questioning of the source(s) of information you receive and taking *their* biases and special interests into account as you assess accuracy.

Successful people are thinkers. Thinking enables them to:

- **Make the future *better* than the past.** This prompts what we call progress. The secret of common people who achieve uncommon results is that they think before they act.
- **Sacrifice *now* to avoid dependence later.** Delayed gratification is still gratification. Learn to have pa-

tience, to *extend* your pleasure over a longer period of time.

- *Prepare* **for the change that will be inevitable.** Agreement is spelled with four letters: B-E-N-D. The best way to impede your own success is to remain inflexible—unbending—unwilling to accept new ideas, new technologies, new approaches to your life.

- **Learn to** *compromise* **to account for the legitimate needs of others.** The smallest supportive action toward an associate is better than the grandest intention. We are judged primarily on the basis of what we *do*, not on what we *intended* to do. Two people are compatible at home when they can enjoy each other's company in silence; two people are compatible at work when each supplies what the other needs.

- **Learn self-discipline.** We all know the tragic consequences of famous individuals who have failed to follow this advice: Marilyn Monroe, whose career ended in suicide; Elvis Presley, who dissipated himself to an early grave; John Belushi, who gave in to the lure of drugs; Magic Johnson, who fell victim to HIV; and President Bill Clinton, whose moral negligence, infatuation with women, and lying nearly took his presidency into collapse.

Those who fail to learn these lessons eventually discover that they have missed out on the benefits of enduring values over short-term goals. By living only for today, they fail to acquire the lasting skills they will need to see them through tomorrow. They fail to learn the benefits of adaptability and flexibility. They condemn themselves to a life of long-term insecurity. And worst of all, they reject the joys and satisfactions of reciprocated affection, respect, and love.

Becoming successful requires taking calculated risks. Life itself is a risk. Nobody has ever been completely safe, completely risk-free. We are *all* required to take risks virtually every single day of our lives. Those who do so most wisely are those who gain the most from them.

Why Losers Lose

Many people fail to succeed for two rather simple reasons:

1. They set their sights too high, causing them to strive for unreachable goals.
2. They simply *do not BELIEVE in themselves strongly enough.*

You do not have to envision yourself as superhuman, but you must have a confident, realistic assessment of your own potential.

Unlike success, which only tends to confirm the positive side of your actions, failure teaches you to examine yourself, examine what you are doing, examine *why* and *how* you are doing it. From that process, important new lessons are learned.

There are ways to reinforce your confidence—your belief in yourself—and they are not difficult.

- **Get positive reinforcement from your friends, family, teachers, or coworkers**—anyone you can honestly depend upon to find and sustain the *positive*, rather than the *negative*, things in your life. Shy away from people who are constantly "looking for the hole in the donut." Associate with the people who are aware of—and impressed by—the positive elements in what you do.

- **Be aware** of the self-serving comments of those who have no ideas of their own.
- **When listening to the evaluations** of people you can trust to be honest, do not listen solely for the things you want to hear, but listen with equal care to constructive criticisms.
- **Make a conscious effort to encourage** *yourself*. Think of yourself as a winner, not as a loser. Make a mental list of all the things that you accomplished yesterday, not the things that you *didn't* get done. Set your sights just *a little bit higher* after each achievement, and then begin again. *Reward* your self for jobs well done.
- **Keep a scrapbook of your achievements.** Include such things as congratulatory letters, newspaper clippings, certificates, awards, and other evidence of your achievements. Frame some and hang them where others can see them.
- **Give yourself the benefit of the doubt.** Nobody can live their entire life on a "high." What you need to do when a "low" occurs is to avoid shouldering a ton of self-doubt, guilt, blame, or responsibility from it. Tell yourself that you have done your best, that you will *continue* to do your best, and that things eventually will turn around in your favor.

- **Avoid trying to find somebody else to blame for your shortcomings.** It will not make you feel better about yourself. If anything, it probably will add to your burden of guilt. Understand that the test of your worth lies in your ability to put negatives behind you rather than your ability to dwell on them. Realize that you will make mistakes, *and so will everyone around you.*

- **Seek outside activities that can help you to recognize your self-worth.** People need to do things *outside* their work—things to rejuvenate themselves, to provide a fresh perspective, and to allow their minds to pursue other interests. Activities with the family often suffice. If not, take up a hobby, a sport, or an opportunity to work with some local charity. Whatever you choose, your participation will invariably reinforce your feeling of self-worth and will help you to become more aware of your special competencies. In spite of their dedication, workaholics seldom reach their full potential. Why? Because they usually confuse working longer with working smarter.

- **What you see is what you get.** People who suffer from low self-esteem often show it in the way they look. Rumpled, mismatched clothing, poorly groomed hair, run-down shoes—all are reflections of an individual who doesn't care. Stand before a mirror and ask yourself, "Does this person reflect self-confidence, capability, assuredness, a desire to succeed?" If the answer is yes, all that remains is to go out and DO it.

To discover how people really feel about you, find out how they describe you to a friend. If you are truly exceptional, let that discovery be made—and voiced—by others.

> ## *The person who graduates and stops learning is not educated.*

Occasionally, it seems as if our lives no longer belong to us—that outside forces such as our families, our employers, the competition, the government, even "fate" have all of the control and there's nothing we can do about it. That's wrong!

When you fall into that mindset, you're giving up. You're trying to find somebody or something to blame for your lack of achievement. Instead of faulting a specific individual, it's also tempting to transfer blame for our "helplessness" to something that's faceless and nameless, but the result is the same.

Perhaps you can't change the circumstances in which you currently find yourself, but you *can* change the way in which you react to it. Instead of trying to find something to blame for your situation, look for a constructive way to deal with it. Look hard enough, and you will find one. That's the day you will begin to take control of your life.

> ### *Find the enemies in your life and ignore them. Find the fears in your life and face them. Find the weaknesses in your life and avoid them. Find the strengths in your life and capitalize on them.*

Traveling Light: The Simpler the Better

Believing in yourself and your abilities allows you to travel through life without carrying a great deal of excess baggage.

Look upon your life and your career as a journey. It is important to take along everything that you will need, yet you must still condition yourself not to overpack. Careful planning *before you depart* can save you a great deal of time, work, and expense later.

By thinking ahead, you can be sure that you're better prepared to meet the day's challenges, but not overburdened with unnecessary concerns.

- Plan ahead, but be flexible. Be prepared to make adjustments.
- Ultimately, what is important is the *process:* the *way* in which you plan to achieve the goal that you're after. When you set your own targets, you usually attain them.

Why Bad Things Happen to Good People

Bad things happen to all of us. Good people are no exception.

Learn to look upon a setback as a singular event, just one of many that contribute to making up your life. If a friend suffers some sort of a setback, don't dwell upon the setback; instead, think about all the wonderful things that have happened to them over the years.

Paul J. Hoenmans, retired Executive vice president of Mobil Corporation, believes that people who have come from a less affluent background make more reliable, more stable employees.

"They're more focused on success and on getting the things out of life that they never had when they were younger," says Hoenmans.

> **Whether you think you can or think you can't—you are right.—Henry Ford**

When setbacks do occur:

First, look at your options. What can you do to minimize the setback or to use it to your advantage? Who do you know that can give you some sound advice? How much time do you have to prevent it from becoming a major catastrophe?

Second, see how much you can learn by studying your options. Why did the setback occur? In other words, try to learn as much from it as you can.

Unacceptable Guilt

Too often, conscientious people feel obligated to assume the responsibility for everything that goes wrong, whether or not they have been instrumental in causing it. That's foolish.

Assuming the blame for your actions is a sign of maturity. Learning from those mistakes is essential for growth. But to take on a heavy burden of guilt is not only non-productive, it is self-defeating.

Those who live in fear of making a mistake will never take a chance, will never run a risk, will never try something new. They are much more likely to repeat their mistakes and compound their failings.

> ### *Courage is strengthened with use.*

Learn to welcome the next challenge, not to fear it. Be confident that, when the time comes, you will be capable of making the right decisions. Discover the ways to turn small adversities into major opportunities.

Above all, learn to be your own best friend. If you don't, who will?

Get a Life

The most significant question regarding success is: Has it made you happy?

- **How do you feel about yourself?** Comfortable? Proud? Eager to face a new day?
- **How do the members of your family, your friends, your business associates feel about you?** Are they happy about your good fortune, or are they envious of you? Do they cherish your company, or do they seek to avoid you?
- **Do you see your work as exciting, challenging, rewarding?** Or would you avoid it if you could?

To most people, happiness entails having time to spend with your spouse and children. Being able to "smell the roses" instead of the exhaust fumes. Being in a position to enjoy a leisurely meal without having to dash off to an airport.

The things you feel you *must* do to achieve success are not the things that define happiness.

There are many forms of success and many definitions of happiness. The challenge is to find the best *combination* of the two.

CHAPTER 8

Victim of Success

Motivation is a two-edged sword. On the positive side, it can spur you onward to attain your full potential. On the negative side, it can get out of control . . . become obsessive . . . a force causing you to lose all sense of proportion.

It is widely recognized that many people are *under*-motivated, but is it possible to be *over*-motivated? Consider President Clinton, whose obsession with the power of the Presidency seems to have thrown everything else in his life into utter chaos—his family, his relationships with friends and coworkers, his moral and ethical values, his sense of duty and responsibility.

In Clinton's case, and in a number of others, an obsession with success sometimes results in a condition of self-sabotage. The individual becomes capable of damaging himself far more than any competitor possibly could.

Fortunately, these people are the exception. Far more often, an individual intent upon attaining success is inclined to set goals *too low*. It's like the child's tale about a little Indian boy whose father tells him to aim his arrow toward the stars. "It may not reach them," he says, "but at least your arrow will go higher than if you aimed at a lower target."

As we set objectives in life, we must be sure to surround ourselves with the family, friends, and coworkers who can and will help us attain them. When we have this support, we tend to work harder and more effectively, and we are happier. It is when we feel alone or unprotected that uncertainties, desperation, and sorrow begin to prevail.

> *If you can't be happy in your work,*
> *you may never know what it is.*

Addiction to success can become a state of bondage. Real freedom results only from an *absence* of addiction to *anything*.

All too often, people who become suddenly successful find themselves isolated, lonely, exposed, vulnerable. That need not be true. It *should* not be true. Success should bring an ever-widening circle of friends and supporters. People do not tend to desert those who are striving to do well or are working to achieve something they consider beneficial.

> *Success is determined by what you*
> *give, not what you have.*

The standards by which to measure success generally are laid out by the work we engage in. A baseball player, for example, is judged by the number of runs batted in or the number of strikeouts. A politician's success depends on the number of votes produced. A doctor is judged by the number of lives saved. Business executives are known by the profits they have generated, the people they have employed, or the product benefits they have produced.

Success depends on how well we can turn ideas into valuable results that benefit people. You cannot motivate people simply by getting them to adopt *your* values. You must develop the ability to motivate them according to *their own* values.

This requires "selling yourself short." You must put your abilities and your priorities in order. Recognize that you spend more of your time working or getting ready for work than you do with your family, friends, engaging in recreation, or any other form of activity. You must get as much out of your investment in work as you possibly can.

Behold the Naked Monarch

An obsession with success, unfortunately, is often caused by an ugly human temptation: greed. Sometimes it would appear that the obsession with success propels an individual toward greed; sometimes it seems that greed propels them toward an obsession with success. Either way, both conditions are deplorable.

Maybe the best illustration of the consequences of greed is found in the story about King Midas. The king had everything. In addition to an enormous empire, he also had a lovely daughter, who was his pride and joy. But Midas wanted more, and when his wish was granted, he asked that everything he touched be turned to gold. Unfortunately, he realized too late that "everything" also included his beloved daughter, and he lost the very thing he loved most to his unbridled greed.

Greedy individuals ultimately lose in the workplace. Employees emulate a selfish boss and become equally greedy. Key employees leave. Greedy individuals lose friends. Adults lose the respect of their children. Nobody reacts favorably to one who is greedy, yet the affliction continues. Why?

Plenty of excuses and explanations prevail. For example, greedy people tend to explain their actions by telling themselves and others:

"I work hard and I've earned this."
"I should be good to myself."
"I need just a little bit more."
"If I don't take this now, I may not have another chance."
"Nobody is *more* deserving than I am."

> *Dandelions are hated because they are easy to grow. Greedy people are avoided because they are easy to tempt.*

We all want to justify the choices we have made in life. Those who are truly successful become better persons in the eyes and hearts of others, not in their own mind.

Andrew Carnegie Revisited

Andrew Carnegie, the twentieth century's leading philanthropist, believed that the shortest and surest route to success is to surround yourself with good people.

Business leaders must demonstrate skills in three key areas:

1. They must look beyond where they *are* and envision where they *could be* and sh*ould be*. They need to understand not only their own job, but also related functions. They need to understand the markets they serve and the industry(ies) they represent. And, in these times of rapid expansion, they need to understand the world beyond our borders.
2. They must be flexible, willing to change when circumstances change.
3. They need to think long-term.

Resumes and references alone are not the best way to determine whether an applicant is worth hiring. Instead, focus on whether the applicant will shoulder responsibility. What is the evidence? When evidence is lacking, continue your search. Wishing will not make it so.

> *Avoid people whose only evidence of being educated is a diploma.*

Effective people do not develop a positive attitude because they win; they win because they have a positive attitude. This results from the conviction "I am going to do better today than I did yesterday and tomorrow will be even better." Each day becomes a new challenge—a new opportunity to prove yourself and what you can do.

Whole Lotta Cheatin' Goin' On—Don't Get Caught Up In It

Although we don't often think about it, there are two kinds of cheating: You can cheat other people, and you can cheat yourself. You cheat yourself when:

1. You accept something for nothing.
2. You are not honest.
3. You do not give credit where and when it is due.
4. You settle for doing less than your best.
5. You avoid tackling a difficult assignment.
6. You overlook or fail to report illegal acts.

Above all, you cheat yourself when you allow someone else to determine your future.

> *When you reach the mountaintop, be prepared to answer this question: "Who did you bring with you?"*

Don't Let Competition Decide

Don't let competition define you. Define yourself according to what you care about most deeply. If you don't, you're cheating yourself.

Success is not just a matter of individual achievement. It's a "we" thing. Ralph Waldo Emerson observed, "It is impossible for a man to be cheated by anyone but himself." A lot of people would argue that statement, but consider this: The reason most people get cheated is because they're attempting to get something for nothing, and an opportunist lures them into a trap. Were it not for greed, would the ruse work? Almost certainly not.

> *There are two things to aim at in life: first, to get what you want; and, after that, to enjoy it. Only the wisest achieve the second.—Logan Smith*

When Greed Prevails

Regardless of how damaging it may be, we can't ignore the fact that greed often takes an upper hand in our lives. Why? Because it frequently provides a necessary shove to get us moving. It can definitely be a strong, driving force in pushing us off of dead center and into action.

Impatience is can be good or bad. It can be self-defeating if you seize upon a solution to a problem prematurely. It can cause you to settle for a result that is far short of what might be attained if you had taken more time. It can create ill will and can be almost as negative in its impact as greed.

Broadcaster Rush Limbaugh believes it is not wise to set out with the intention of earning a lot of money. Rather, he says, you should work on something important and meaningful and do it exceptionally well. If you succeed, the chances are good that money will follow.

The late Erma Bombeck had an unsurpassed way of making complex matters simple and funny. Here's how she expressed her concept of what success is all about:

"I always had a dream that when I am asked to give an accounting of my life to a higher court, it will go like this: 'So, empty your pockets. What have you got left of your life? Any dreams that were unfulfilled? Any unused talent that we gave you when you were born that you still have left? Any unsaid compliments or bits of love that you haven't spread around?' And I will answer, I've nothing to return. I spent everything you gave me."

If you are looking down today Erma, thank you!

CHAPTER 9

What Good Is Experience?

Experience is the best teacher, you say. But is it? Sometimes yes, sometimes no. It all depends on you. Too often what we call experience is nothing but repetition. To be more valuable we must not only *learn* from experience, but also *apply* it and improve. Experience can be good if:

- **It has prepared you for today.** Looking backward is appropriate only for historians.
- **You are comfortable with change.** Those who resist change get nowhere.
- **You welcome new ideas.** If you don't have new ideas, the other guy wins.
- **You scan the horizon for competitive advantage.** No one else can make you more competitive.
- **You never stop exploring.** Avoiding failure is not the same as success.

- **You change wrongs before they become habits.** The adage "Nothing ventured—nothing gained" has never been more true.
- **You learn to simplify, not complicate.** Those who try to impress with complicated solutions often want to see others fail.
- **You can apply it to current problems.** Knowledge alone is useless. To make a difference it must be applied.
- **You are committed to renewal.** Resistance to change is a career killer.
- **You use it to stretch to new heights.** There is no growth while you are protecting yourself from criticism.

Good experiences are building blocks that enable you to create your own future. People who learn to define good experience have laid the foundation for becoming leaders. They are rarely victims. They set the pace.

Gaining *good* experience requires initiative. You can't wait for someone else to provide it. You must risk making mistakes. You must challenge old ways. You must not be afraid of criticism.

Those who make steady, rather than sensational, progress are disciplined. They don't think in terms of miracles or even unexpected breakthroughs. They plug away, constantly alert for ways to use what they have learned to move on to the next step. Experience can be bad if:

- **Your skills are out of date.** Who is to blame when a low-skilled person is laid off or replaced: the individual or the employer?

- **You are locked into past habits.** It is always dangerous to be more concerned about appearance than substance.
- **You resist change.** Don't let yourself be concerned by what hasn't worked before. If you don't believe that change is inevitable, you've been in a deep coma.
- **You keep reliving "the good old days."** Those who are constantly alert for bad news usually find it.
- **You fear making mistakes.** Remember, to avoid failure is to limit accomplishment.
- **You apply old solutions to new problems.** Nothing surpasses the disillusionment of a person whose "tried-and-true, time-tested" method fails.
- **You waste energy on regrets.** Doom and gloom are infectious. Don't spread the disease.
- **You seek comfort in repetition.** The same old ways simply are not good enough in a society in which the pace is set by high tech.
- **You dwell too long on past accomplishments.** Typically, people who live in the past are out of touch with the present and don't have much of a future.
- **You have followed the wrong people.** When you paddle your own canoe, you can do the steering.

Sure, you can learn from bad experiences. But why create them? Why even allow them to happen if they can be prevented? Bad experiences should not be glossed over. They must be faced and dealt with. If you choose to blame someone else for your bad experiences, you can, but you will be the ultimate loser.

To check up on the quality of your current experiences, ask yourself these questions:

- What are the long-term consequences of this?
- If I continue on this path, will I be better or worse off?
- What am I learning that is new?

Unless you are truly happy as a specialist, consider broadening your career options by adding new skills that will keep you in demand. Whether you are comfortable with it or not, the best advice that can be given to young people is "Never forget, it's a what-have-you-done-for-me-lately-world"!

The keys to minimizing the impact of bad experiences and maximizing benefit from the good ones are *awareness* and *initiative*. Awareness of the above clues will put you on the right track. Initiative to practice the good and eliminate the bad will keep you moving ahead.

Experience provides the building blocks on which we construct our lives. Each new experience serves as a base for another, and another, and another.

Those with few experiences usually live more limited lives. Those who amass many sometimes construct grand monuments to their achievements.

In the not-too-distant past, experience with an employer had a great deal to do with status. Longevity was very important; it indicated loyalty, dependability, dedication. This is not so today. Now, an individual with a long history within a company usually falls into one of two categories: (1) strong upward mobility or (2) dead-ended in his or her job.

People are much more mobile these days. If they can't reach a specific plateau within a predetermined time-frame, they move on. If they are particularly "hot," they are constantly being recruited by other companies. Either way, staying with one company for a long time is unlikely.

> *When chickens quit quarreling over their food, they usually find that there is enough for all of them*

Certainly, experience can hardly produce much benefit without action and thought. In the long run, our lives are the sumtotal of our experiences, and those begin at the moment of our birth.

It is interesting to consider what happens to people as they grow older. Go to a group of kindergarten children, for example, and ask them if they can draw, or sing, or dance, and *every one of them* will answer "yes." Ask them to show you, and every one of them will do so.

Go to the same group of people after they have reached college age, and ask them the same questions. Most of them will say "no," and the few who don't will express certain qualifications. "I can draw a little, but . . ." "I *like* to sing, but . . ." "My dancing is terrible."

Why is that? What happens between the ages of five and twenty? Does "growing up" really mean "shrinking down"?

Does the same thing happen in the workplace? Are employees becoming less and less motivated to increase their effectiveness instead of trying to grow and improve? Do they become happy to just "get by" and let their pay raises be automatic?

Societal changes have a profound effect on the workplace.

Effects on the markets are well known and frequently documented, but effects on the workforce are equally meaningful. The impact of the computer is a notable example.

Another example is the increasing number of "latchkey children"—children whose parents are both working. Unlike children in the past, today's children are forced to accept more responsibility *at an earlier age*. Does this mean that they will mature at an earlier age? Enter the workforce better prepared to deal with responsibility? More strongly motivated?

Only time will tell, but it has already been suggested that the aging of this group of self-sufficient youngsters may have a direct effect on the ever-increasing trend toward entrepreneurialism in America. More people, it seems, prefer to be their own boss than to work in a large, well-structured corporation.

Thanks to the computer and the Internet, there is virtually nothing that cannot be accessed and learned, and virtually nobody who cannot be contacted, in a matter of minutes. So there can be no doubt that the best means to ensure future success is to position yourself to find out what you need to know *quickly*.

John Shriber, just twenty-two years old at the time, launched Apartment Source in New York City in 1995. For a fee, Shriber's customers received lists of available apartments via e-mail. The business generated $3,000 worth of business on the first day! Shriber says he wasn't surprised by the success of his company, he had just underestimated how successful it would be. There is absolutely no doubt that America is rapidly moving toward an information-based economy.

Sometimes experience is a handicap.

Example: Peter Gruber, chairman of Mandalay Entertainment, learned that lesson while filming the movie "Gorillas in the Mist."

The original plan was to film the picture using more than two hundred animals in the jungles of Rwanda at an altitude of ten thousand feet. It was a frightfully expensive plan, and one that was saddled with many complications. Rwanda, for example, was on the verge of revolution. And *nobody* had the slightest idea how to go about teaching a gorilla to "act" in front of a camera, much less to follow a script.

During a conference one day, an inexperienced young intern came up with a workable solution: "Send a crack cinematographer into the jungle with a ton of film," she said. "Let him shoot as much footage of gorillas as possible, and then *write the script around the actions of the gorillas*, rather than expecting the gorillas to perform according to a previously-written script."

Result: The film was finished at a total cost of $20 million—*half* of the original budget—because an open-minded, inexperienced intern was able to look for a solution in a very *unorthodox* way.

> *Experience is the name everyone gives to their mistakes.* —*Oscar Wilde*

Dependence Is Not Dependable

Example: Josephine Esther Mentzer, the youngest of nine children, was born in Queens, New York. The family lived above a hardware store. As a child, "Esty" sold face creams made by her

Hungarian uncle in a stable behind the house. After a stab at acting, she married Joseph Lauter, whom she later divorced and then remarried. She and her husband formed a business to market Esty's face creams.

Esty's grade-school principal misspelled her first name . . . and it stuck. Estee and Joseph changed their last name from Lauter to Lauder. Today everyone knows the name Estee Lauder.

Planning Puts Experience in Focus

Without a plan, we are dependent upon others to tell us what to do, when to do it, and, all-too-often, even how to do it. The first step toward independence—and success—is to develop the ability to plan.

Planning means setting goals in three areas: Short term, intermediate, and long term. Short-term goals are those that you can reasonably expect to attain in days or weeks. Intermediate goals may take months—even a year—to accomplish. And long-term goals are those toward which all of the short- and intermediate-term goals are directed: goals that, realistically, will take longer than a year—maybe three to five years of dedicated effort and resources.

Your goals should be reasonable—things you can genuinely expect to accomplish within the time-frame provided for them. They must be specific. They should be in writing, and you should review them often to maintain your focus. When circumstances require it, they should be modified to accommodate unexpected changes.

Your plan should *always* be your road map . . . your point of focus. But never regard it as rigid and inflexible. Whenever necessary, expect to modify it—especially when circumstances beyond your control make it unworkable

With a solid plan, you will not be dependent upon other people to make your career decisions. You will be in a position to create your future.

Example: Phil Knight took charge of his future when he recognized the increased interest in running and jogging that was sweeping the nation. Advised by his college track coach that American-made shoes were inferior to some of the shoes made abroad, Knight thought he saw a business opportunity. He and his coach invested $500 each to buy three hundred pairs of Japanese shoes, and the firm now known as Nike was born.

> *Experience is good only if it prevents you from making the same mistake.*

Example: Age, like gender, is no longer a deterrent to someone with an ambition and some drive.

At the age of fouteeen, the son of a Seattle lawyer took an interest in computers and began to write some of his own programs. At fifteen, he and a friend developed some software that could analyze traffic patterns and formed a company that produced $20,000 in sales during its first year. At seventeen, he dropped out of high school for a year to computerize the power grid that controls all of the electricity in the city of Vancouver, Washington. Two years later, while he was a sophomore in college, he learned about the development of the world's first PC . . . and discovered that there was no software for the system.

The young man and his friend contacted the computer manufacturer and offered to develop the necessary software. For three weeks, the two worked out of a cheap motel room . . . and successfully programmed the company's PC. Instead of returning to college, Bill Gates and his friend, Paul Allen, formed Microsoft Corporation. Today he is the richest man in the world.

Example: Stephen Wozniak and Steven Jobs, who, while holding down regular jobs, invested $1,300 in a company they created to produce minicomputers. In the first year, their revenues amounted to $77,000. Three years later, when sales had climbed to $117 million, Apple Computer went public.

Example: A blacksmith's son in postwar Japan invested $3,300 to form a company that would make motorcycles from old military parts that had been abandoned after the war. Within two years, the company had five thousand dealers throughout Japan, and ten years after that the company introduced its motorcycles to the American market. Today, Soichiro Honda's company is the world leader in sales of motorcycles and automobiles combined.

Honda had found a way to create his own opportunity.

No Shortcuts

It would be foolhardy today to advise anybody not to get as much formal education as possible. It would be equally foolhardy to say that you *cannot* succeed simply because you do not have an exceptional education. History has proven this to be false. William Lear, founder of Lear Jet, dropped out of school in the eighth grade. Carl H. Lindner, founder of American Financial Company, was a high-school drop-out.

> ## *A wise man will make more opportunities than he finds.*

Example: It would be equally false to suggest that America's most successful individuals moved to the very top on their first effort. Most suffered many setbacks before they finally succeeded. Bud Hadfield is a classic example.

Hadfield became an entrepreneur at the age of twelve, when he used a small hand-fed printing press to produce a little neighborhood newspaper. But instead of moving onward and upward from there, Hadfield got into trouble in high school and was expelled for fighting. Lacking a high school diploma, he went into the Merchant Marines, then tried the egg business and the ice cream business, both of which failed.

Borrowing his mother's car, Hadfield moved away, lived in a mobile home, and paid a widow $2,500 for a small print shop. The 18 x 20-foot shop had no running water, and Hadfield had to use the bathroom at a corner service station.

For the next half-dozen years, he took time out to serve as executive assistant to the Mayor of Houston, allowing his print shop to decline badly. When he returned to printing, he found that new technology had rendered his old equipment obsolete, but he recognized the potential in the newly introduced direct-imaging camera and small offset press. Hadfield sold his old equipment, moved to a new location, and opened his first Kwik-Kopy Center. Today Kwik-Kopy is a worldwide enterprise.

Example: Two other young men in their mid-twenties learned a similar lesson. They lived in a rich California wine-growing region, surrounded by vineyards, and thought they would like to go into the wine-producing business. But America was just coming out of Prohibition, American palates were much more attuned to beer than to wine, and there was another major hurdle—the brothers knew absolutely nothing about how wine is made. So Ernest and Julio Gallo went to the Modesto Public Library, withdrew some books on wine-making, and went into business—subsequently becoming the largest wine-producing company in the world.

> *To know the road ahead, ask those coming back.—Chinese Proverb*

Use It or Lose It

The qualities of courage, dependability, flexibility, integrity, judgment, and respect for others are all critical to the task of managing people. They are not related to the typical characteristics of the volatile, inventive, dynamic entrepreneurs who often spot, isolate, and develop the ideas upon which companies are built.

Hiring someone capable of managing the day-to-day functions associated with running a company is far smarter than making a series of potentially disastrous mistakes.

> *More valuable than ability is the ability to recognize ability.*

Finding motivated, well-trained personnel to help operate a business is a difficult task. Some companies look for their key personnel outside the firm, while others are constantly attempting to train and promote people from within.

Example: Michael Parks, CEO of the Revere Group, a Chicago technology consulting firm, believes in career planning. At the beginning of each year, every employee sits down with a company-assigned mentor who has been chosen for people skills, knowledge of the company, and knowledge of the industry. Together, they develop the employee's plan for personal development during the year ahead. The plan usually spells out (a) how the employee will spend two required weeks of career training and (b) what progress the employee needs to make to receive a promotion or to change jobs. Each employee then receives a quarterly update on his progress and engages in a periodic review with his mentor.

Parks' program has done wonders for the company's employee-retention figures . . . and has resulted in numerous employee advancements within the firm.

> ### *Don't be an alarmist, unless there's a fire.*

Intuition has always been extremely dangerous in business, and it's inexcusable today. Solid, timely business information is within an arm's reach everywhere—and it's free for the taking. We have the library, the Internet, countless government agencies, and trade associations that have been formed to serve literally every known industry.

From such free-for-the-asking sources, brothers Anthony and Michael Caito and their friend Matthew Martha not long ago learned that 51 percent of the food prepared in today's restaurants *is eaten off premises.* Using this information and an initial investment of $10,000, the three young men formed Restaurants on the Run, a company devoted to delivering food between the restaurant and its customers. Their company allowed its customers to compete with such home-delivery pioneers as Peter Piper Pizza, yet not have to create, staff, and manage a delivery service of their own. Within seven years, Restaurants on the Run was generating $6 million in income annually.

> *The more we memorize,
> the less we think.*

In a knowledge-based economy, learning is the key ingredient for success. If you want to build a business that will grow, create a culture that treasures learning. If you want to succeed, maintain your hunger to learn—and join an organization that encourages and nurtures that interest.

Send Me In, Coach

It is desire, rather than capital, that stimulates a successful business. It is not enough to have a brilliant idea and to provide suitable financing; success also requires dedication and hard work. William Hewlett and David Packard started Hewlett-Packard with just $538 between them.

But how can you know that you're really ready to move up the ladder within the company? You will be ready to move up when the situation falls under one of the following categories:

- When you see an opportunity that you are sure you can exploit.
- When you have tested your readiness under similar circumstances.
- When your performance level exceeds your confidence level.
- When your confidence level is based on the completion of many difficult assignments.
- When your results exceed your boss's expectations.
- When your boss sees a need you can fill because you have already done it.
- When you are recommended by someone who has a lot to lose if you don't make it.
- When you are sure you can replace "wishing on the beach" with "achieving in the field."
- When your achievement level is acknowledged by other players.
- When your performance speaks for itself.

One of the best ways to get ahead is to make sure you're the person who's always first to volunteer for a challenging assignment.

> ## *Only a fool learns unused skills.*

Four major issues confront all employers as the world enters a new century:

1. **Attracting and retaining the best employees** *continuously*. With competition growing tougher and education standards falling rapidly, you will need to find innovative ways to get and keep effective people.
2. **Developing a competitive advantage.** Anyone who aspires to have a competitive advantage in the information age must know where and how to get information *before* it is needed.
3. **Finding advisors to help define a plan of action, determine expected outcomes, and analyze resource requirements** *realistically*.
4. **Forming alliances that will strengthen** *both* **parties.**

Those who gain the most from experience must first learn simply to *overcome inertia*. The sooner you begin to move toward your goal, the greater the likelihood of getting there.

Curtis Carlson was one of five children. His parents were poor, hard-working Swedish immigrants. Carlson worked at one job or another from the time he was nine—caddying at the local golf club, delivering newspapers, driving a truck, selling advertising. He developed a strong work ethic early on.

Carlson's first entrepreneurial effort was the formation of

Gold Bond Stamp Company, a competitor of S&H Green Stamps. Subsequently, the Carlson Companies have expanded to include TGI Friday's and Country Kitchen restaurants, Radisson Hotels, Ask Mr. Travel, and some six dozen other corporations.

Get the Wind at Your Back

.This is the real key to getting maximum benefit from experience. You must give yourself as much advantage as you can. I believe this so much that I named my publishing company the Inside Advantage. Here are the ways to know whether you are positioning yourself for maximum advantage:

- Take every opportunity to learn. Don't be limited to schools with teachers and textbooks. If your parents won't help you, find someone who will—relatives, friends, coworkers. Seek as many people as possible who will take time to listen, share your concerns, and *constructively criticize* your ideas.
- Select friends wisely. Avoid bad company. Guard your reputation. Drop those who develop dangerous habits or want to drag you down to a lower level of aspiration or accomplishment.
- Arrive early and stay late. Distinguish yourself by your conscientiousness. You will soon find that you are usually selected for leadership positions.
- Volunteer for experiences that will stretch you intellectually and test your stability under fire.
- Be picky about where you work, who you work for,

and what you do. Don't let yourself slip into a career selected by someone else or determined by money, location, benefits ,or some other tempting but secondary reason. Do what you like most and are self-motivated to do well without pushing or pulling by someone else.

It's your life—live it!

C H A P T E R   1 0

The Secrets of Self Mastery

Ironically, as more and more Americans seek masters degrees to prove their mastery of a subject, fewer and fewer can claim mastery of themselves. I believe it is time to reexamine our priorities.

Self-mastery is the key to civilized living and lasting personal satisfaction. Without it, the best result is wasted talent, and the worst is criminal behavior.

If you are not in charge of your life, someone else will be. Easier said than done, you say? Sure, but we're not talking about rocket science or astrology here. We're talking about some basic, simple, easy-to-recognize concepts that work in real life.

Here are the ones that have helped me most. You are invited to try them. You prove self-mastery and are worthy of the trust and confidence of others when you:

> **Thrive on less praise than you deserve.** Self-disciplined people create their own incentives, they are not easily discouraged, they do not need constant and continuous reinforcement to make difficult decisions. When you see someone in a position of leadership making an

unpopular decision, you can usually be certain that (1) their self-confidence and persistence has been tested many times, and (2) they believe that they can deal with the severe pressures that accompany an unpopular decision.

Anticipate victory. We must focus on what is required to win and must be at the same time be willing to negotiate to prevent a serious defeat. Those people who are most successful over a long time don't gloat over wins. They move on to the next challenge. Think of it this way: Every hour spent gloating in victory is an hour that is not spent preparing for the next victory. As a matter of fact, gloating is usually self-defeating, because it tends to encourage enemies who can now see your inability to take winning in stride, which is a weakness. Be assured that this is a weakness they will exploit this weakness at the earliest opportunity.

Accept defeat only as a temporary setback. Don't dwell on losses. Learn as much as you can from your setback, and lay plans to move on. You will find that much more can be learned from loss than from victory. Jose Maria Olazabel won the Masters Golf Tournament for the second time in April 1999. It was an exciting come-from-behind victory over the greatest field of golfers in the world. But his most important victory was not on the golf course. Three years before, in 1996, a mysterious disease led some doctors to conclude that Jose might never play golf again—in fact, might never even walk again! How could this happen? Two things brought him back to the top: (1) a change in diagnosis and (2) his unshaking commitment to recovery.

Capitalize on strengths. When you fail to make the best use of your natural gifts and talents, you become your own worst enemy. Before there were computer games, there were board games. Trained as an engineer, Charles B. Darrow also knew something about business, and he knew something about people, as well. Combining his knowledge of the two, he created a board game that included some of the more intriguing elements of real estate, finance, human nature, and chance. He called the game Monopoly. Darrow became a millionaire and was able to retire at the age of forty-six.

Share credit. Selfishness is universally resisted and resented. It is the ultimate evidence that you care little about what happens to other people and are focused exclusively on yourself.

Ideas shared grow as they go.

Understand that admiration and wealth are fleeting. Michael Jordan's mother, Deloris, is credited by most people who know her as being the driving force in their family. "I know I wouldn't have these doors open to me without Michael's achievements," she says. "I'm very humbled and grateful for this. I believe God puts you in this position for a reason. God blessed me with a beautiful family and a famous son, so I could try to help others and share what I have learned as a parent." Mrs. Jordan has helped raise over $7 million through various charities and foundations, most of it for disadvantaged children.

We are judged by what we love.

Sacrifice short-term satisfaction for long-term gain. To illustrate this point, researchers at Stanford University conducted what became known as the "Marshmallow Challenge." They selected a group of four-year-old children and gave each of them two marshmallows. The researchers then instructed the children that they could either eat their marshmallows immediately or wait until later, when a better treat might be offered to them. They left the room for a few minutes and returned to discover that 60 percent of the kids chose immediate gratification and ate their marshmallows right away. Many years later they brought the same group of people together as adults and studied them. The results were very interesting. Those who ate their marshmallows right away had difficulty in sustaining and reaching long-term goals as adults. In addition, the 40 percent of the participants who postponed eating their candy treats had scored significantly higher on the Scholastic Aptitude Test (SAT) than those who did not.

Make yourself needed. The most secure people in the working world are those who can quickly identify the ways they can supplement and complement what others need at work. This keeps them in demand. The story of Tom Sawyer survives because he made work he did not want to do sound like fun. Although he was only twenty years old at the time, Morris (Mo) Siegel had little doubt about what would or would not appeal to his customers. Siegel saw the health-foods fad developing long before many others did and opened a health-food store, where he began to blend a succession of herbal teas. As the business grew, Siegel took on more and more employees, which in turn helped the company to expand even more. Within six years, Celestial Seasonings had made Siegel a millionaire.

Listen to the marketplace and seek family support. When the market needed a fast, reliable delivery system, Frederick W. Smith was listening. He wrote a class paper on it while he was in college. But it wasn't until after Smith had graduated from college and had completed two tours of duty in Vietnam that he decided to act upon his idea. It was an adventuresome undertaking, especially for someone who was still in his mid-twenties, but today Smith's Federal Express is now a multinational, multibillion-dollar company. The cooperation of his family and employees helped Smith get where he is today. Jack Miller got similar support from his family when he set up the Quill Corporation, a company devoted to the sale of office supplies via mail order. Miller's father-in-law provided the initial $2,000 needed to get the business started, an uncle provided office space, and two of his brothers joined the company to handle the accounting, purchasing, and production. Smith and Miller listened to the marketplace and created solid business opportunities. Their friends and family listened to them and gave them the necessary support.

Extend your capability. When Victor Kiam saw that Sperry-Rand Corporation was losing money on its Remington line of electric shavers, he thought he could do better. For one thing, he could see that the company had been top-heavy, overburdened by nearly a hundred non-producing but highly paid executives. Kiam put together a leveraged buyout, took over the firm, used his organizational skills to develop a more efficient management team, and turned the company around in five years.

Expand your mind with continuous new learning experiences. Just like your body, your mind must be exercised regularly to stay in top working condition. Howard Hughes inherited millions and acquired many more, but he became so self centered, paranoid, insecure and deranged, that he died sick, diseased, despised, miserable and alone. His decision to withdraw from the world and become an isolated hermit shut off all avenues for accomplishment. Probably the best place to start for most of us is to accept the challenge of learning how to use a personal computer.

Find a job you enjoy and improve it. It's a big, wide, wonderful world. To stay in a job you don't like simply postpones the satisfactions of working in a situation that is both enjoyable and challenging. Dexter Guillory, for example, has learned how to use nature to his advantage and multiply the income from his rice paddies. In April, Guillory plants rice. In May, when the rice plants are up, he floods the fields and stocks them with crawfish. In September he harvests the rice, and in November he harvests the crawfish. By seeing potential where other rice farmers saw none, Guillory has been able to turn two businesses into one.

Build balanced personal relationships. This means avoiding relationships that are lopsided in favor of one party, even if that party is you. Sam Walton realized the importance of making customers feel welcome and insisted that an employee always be present to greet people as they entered his stores. He featured employees in WalMart advertising. He constantly and consistently asked employees for their ideas about how business could be improved. Every one of these actions, which came so naturally to him, paid off because they were in stark contrast to what his competitors (Sears, Montgomery Ward, and J.C. PenneyJ) were doing.

Quickly disassociate yourself from people who are poor examples of what you want to be. Select only reliable role models who have proven their worthiness over time. This can become a problem for some children. Columnist Bill Mego is advocating a fascinating theory about the recent mass murder of thirteen high-school students in Littleton, Colorado. He writes, "Deep inside, we all know how this occurred, and who should have prevented it. Perhaps the killers' parents were too wrapped up in their careers, material possessions, and other self-indulgences. Perhaps it was something else. Only a parent who is fully engaged in his child's daily life can determine which influences are harmful, where interventions are needed, and when to instruct by example. Without the consistent values only a parent can provide, life can soon appear cynical and arbitrary."

Refuse to engage in self-pity. Take what you have and build on it. Never think of yourself as deprived, disadvantaged, handicapped, or as a victim. Ask first: What are the causes of my condition? What *can* I do about them? What *must* I do about them? When you are tempted to feel sorry for yourself or to believe you are a helpless victim, visit a nursing home, a children's hospital, or a funeral parlor. Don't dwell on past mistakes, use them to avoid future trouble.

> *Self mastery is by far the most important and useful credential to be earned. Are you enrolled?*

About the Author

Roger Fritz is considered one of the country's foremost authorities on Performance Based Management and change requirements for individuals. Organizations from Fortune 500 companies to family-owned businesses have used his advice. Dr. Fritz has served over 300 clients and takes time each month for keynote, workshop and seminar presentations. His features in monthly magazines and weekly columns in business newspapers reach millions of readers. His 32 published books include several best sellers, book-of-the-month selections and award winners.

Roger passionately believes that *life is anticipation* and reveals in many captivating ways how that powerful principle changes lives and prompts success. His presentations feature unique combinations of humor, inspiration, practical advice and the impact of personal accountability.

He is founder (1972) and president of Organization Development Consultants, 1240 Iroquois Drive, Suite 406, Naperville, IL 60563 • Phone: 630-420-7673 • Fax: 630-420-7835 • Email: RFritz3800@aol.com • Website: http://www.rogerfritz.com

Index

ability 4, 8, 53, 60, 81, 106
accountability 64
achievement 40, 51, 62, 65, 80, 93, 109
admiration 115
advantage 51, 71, 95, 111
ambition 7, 19, 55
Angelou, Maya 38
apathy 68
attitude 6,21,54,60, 92

barriers 48
Bennis, Warren 3
blame 24, 64, 81-82
Bombeck, Irma 94
busyness 41-42

career 8, 98
Carlson, Curtis 110
Carnegie, Andrew 91
change, 10, 15, 47, 52, 78, 95, 96, 97
charisma 60
cheating 92, 93
commitment 9, 36, 37, 60, 63, 115
common man 29
competition 21, 48, 75 93, 110
compliments 34
compromise 52, 73, 78
confidence 60, 62, 67, 79, 109, 113

control 36, 39, 44, 51, 82
courage 76, 85
creativity 44, 101
credibility 8, 9

decisions 68, 69, 72, 73
defeat 114
dependence 77, 101

ego 6
enemies 82
excuses 55, 58, 65
experience 23, 95-99, 101, 103

failure 35, 39, 65, 66, 67, 76
fear 32, 47, 75, 76, 82, 84
friendship 51

Gallo, Ernest & Julio 105
Gandhi, Mahatma 75
Gaston, Mack 33
Gates, Bill 104
goals 37, 51, 102
gratification 116
greatness 75
greed 89-90, 93
guilt 13, 45, 80, 84,

Hadfield, Bud 105

happiness 19, 20, 32, 60, 85, 86, 88
helping 5, 36
Holtz, Lou   27
Honda, Soichiro 104
Hoover, Herbert 29
hunkering 69

ideas 48, 115
information 23, 58, 64, 77, 100, 110
intuition 107

Johnson, Robert 35-36
Jordan, Deloris 115-116
Jordan, Michael 115
Judd, Naomi 66

Kapoor, John 18
Kiam, Victor 118
Koch, Ed 67
Kroc, Ray 28

leadership 47, 113-114
learning 36, 51, 59, 108, 118
Limbaugh, Rush 94
listening 72, 80
losers 24, 48, 79
love 116

managing 47, 64, 106
meetings 52, 56
Melman, Rich 24
memorize 108
mentor 51
Miller, Jack 117
minutia 51, 54
mistakes 31, 54, 59, 81, 97, 101, 103, 106
motivation 30, 37, 47, 87
Moyer, Jamie 68

objectivity 4, 36
opportunity 31, 105

Page, Patti 1
patience 31, 93
performance 15, 37, 55, 72
perseverance 36
persistence 28, 29, 37, 63, 73, 114
personal history 34
planning 83, 102, 107
positive thinking 20
power 58, 63, 72
practice 69, 98
praise 64
presentations 53
pride 7, 35
problems 51, 58
promises 51
promotion 107, 109
prompter 61

rainmakers 47, 61, 62
referenceable people 42-43
renewal 29, 96, 122
reputation 42, 51, 111
respect 18, 35, 36, 51, 106
responsibility 18, 25, 33, 65, 91, 100
risk 57, 61, 79, 84, 96
role models 119-120

sacrifice 28, 77, 116
security 67, 69, 79, 116
self mastery 113, 120
self pity 120
self worth 81
self discipline 78, 113
selfishness 115
Siegel, Mo 117
simplicity 41, 54, 70, 83, 96

skills 4, 51, 68, 91, 96, 98, 110
Smith, Fred 117
Sony Corp. 28
strengths 34, 82, 115
stress 46, 70
subjectivity 36
success 3, 5, 17, 21, 22, 28, 29, 32,
    34, 37, 50, 66, 67, 72, 79, 85-90,
    93, 94, 100

thinking 41, 44, 76-77, 101
Thomas, Dave 24-26
time use 35, 38, 53, 58
truths 56, 58

values 18, 28, 51
victory 114
vision 38, 47, 50

Walton, Sam 119
weaknesses 51, 63, 82
wealth 115
Welch, Jack 47
winners 56, 67, 80
wisdom 44
Wooden, John 50
work 35, 39, 41, 88, 109

Additional Information

For more information about Dr. Roger Fritz's consulting and pre-sentation topics or for a catalog of books, audio tapes, CD-ROMS, reprints, software and other products, contact:

Organization Development Consultants
Phone: 630.420.7673
Fax: 630.420.7835
Email: RFritz3800@aol.com
Website: http://www.rogerfritz.com